THE
READER'S COMPANION
TO
DANTE'S *DIVINE COMEDY*

THE
READER'S COMPANION
TO
DANTE'S *DIVINE COMEDY*

Angelo A. De Gennaro
Loyola Marymount University
Los Angeles, California

Philosophical Library
New York

All the excerpts from the *Divine Comedy* used in this book have been translated by John Ciardi and are reprinted by arrangement with New American Library. The excerpts from the *Inferno* are copyrighted 1954 and 1982 by Mr. Ciardi; the excerpts from the *Purgatorio* are copyrighted 1957, 1959, 1960, and 1961 by Mr. Ciardi; and the excerpts from the *Paradiso* are copyrighted 1961, 1965, 1967, and 1970 by Mr. Ciardi. The author is grateful for permission to quote.

Library of Congress Cataloging-in-Publication Data

De Gennaro, Angelo A., 1919-
The reader's companion to Dante's Divine comedy.

Bibliography: p.
1. Dante Alighieri, 1265-1321. Divina commedia.
I. Dante Alighieri, 1265-1321. Divina commedia.
II. Title.
PQ4390.D34   1986   851'.1   85-21413
ISBN 0-8022-2502-0

To Ann, Gina and Laura

TABLE OF CONTENTS

7

PURGATORIO

PARADISO

FOREWORD

The vast bibliography on Dante and his works has never exhausted the field of inquiry, and scholars and critics can always find something new to say, particularly of the *Divine Comedy*, the poem "to which heaven and earth set their hand." The Poem has proved to be a continual source of reflection and a boundless field for discoveries that fit every generation or period of human history. This *Reader's Companion to Dante's "Divine Comedy"* is yet another modest addition to the huge work of exegesis, scholarship, and esthetic interpretation covering more than six centuries of Dante studies. It is obviously meant to be a study guide, a companion, for students; eventually, however, it goes beyond the limits of mere guide and offers, in a straightforward and simple form, some personal insights that attest to a long familiarity with the great poem.

Great works of literature mean much more than they say. Thus, they are difficult to read with prompt and full understanding. They require much thought and reflection and many long hours of research before they unveil their hidden meanings. Great writers are at times discouraging to approach because of the complexity and depth and richness of vision. The function of "experts" is to pave the way for inexperienced readers with appropriate elucidations and commentaries on the text. Their work, of course, must never be a substitute for the direct reading of the text itself!

Unquestionably the *Divine Comedy* is one of the most difficult works to understand thoroughly. While one may enjoy reading the beautiful lyrical passages, most of the poem often remains obscure. The innumerable historical, philosophical, and theological references, the various levels of meaning, and the intricate symbolism, create an almost unmanageable complexity. Dante is a supreme poet, but he is also a learned scholar. Although he fuses his scholarship in the fire of his inspiration, the learned quality of the poem is not attenuated. The *Divine Comedy* is a compendium of medieval culture, which Dante's mind encompasses fully: science, philosophy, theology, astrology, political doctrine, religious spirit, human ideals, are all there to form the gigantic architecture of the poem to which the passions of the poet give life and movement.

The work was meant to be a monument to Beatrice, the woman Dante lived in his youth and whom he transfigured into his spiritual guide. At the end of his *Vita Nuova*, in which he narrates his love for her soon after her untimely death, he promises to speak no more until he can say something worthy of her. Between his youthful *Vita Nuova* and the composition of the great poem, Dante devoted himself to serious studies of philosophy and science, abandoning the poetry of the "Sweet New Style." In order to write of Beatrice "what had never been said of any woman," he had to compose a philosophical work, for only philosophy, which at that time comprised all forms of human and divine knowledge, was endowed with a dignity worthy of his lady. Philosophy and science, a spiritual and natural conception of the universe, became his great ambition. He thought love poetry unbecoming to his age and fame. Dante would certainly not undermine poetry, but his own would be learned; it would contain serious teaching—the teaching of eternal truth. He would use poetry simply as adornment; the substance of it would be philosophy. His turning to substantive learning is evident in his unfinished *Banquet*, a work conceived as an encyclopedic treatise in fifteen books—the first book to serve as a general introduction, and the other fourteen as commentaries to as many allegorical compositions. Although the work may appear as the continuation of his *Vita Nuova*, the "gentle lady" becomes now the symbol of philosophy. The *Banquet* is a feast of science, learning, philosophy, attesting to the vast knowledge of the poet and his scholarly accomplishments. The high learning displayed in the *Banquet* somehow foretold the scholarly nature of the *Divine Comedy*. All Dante's intellectual acquisitions found their way into the *Divine Comedy*, making it one of the most complex poems in western literature.

Its learned complexity and obscurity were, to a large extent, deliberate. As Dante explained in the *Banquet*, an easy book would arouse contempt. The intricacy of its design is apparent in the self-exegesis he gave in a letter to Can Grande della Scala to whom the *Paradiso* was dedicated. In eleven pages he unfolds the architecture of the entire poem in its many-faceted aspects and meanings, its purpose, and the method by which it was carried out. The poem as described by its author is a work of instruction and, therefore, a work to study, to labor upon; it was not meant for futile delight. Easy works, to Dante's mind, would become trivial and unworthy of his high aims. No one but specialists can profitably get through the *Divine Comedy* without the aid of commentaries, notes, and guides. Despite the fact that Dante, in order to bring the work closer to popular understanding wrote in vernacular rather than Latin, the poem by its own nature remains nonetheless obscure to the unaided reader, who often cannot go beyond the literal meaning, that is, the narrative of the journey. In fact, the labor of interpretation and explanation began the year following the poet's death with the commentary on the *Inferno* by Dante's son, Jacopo Alighieri (1322), and has continued unabated throughout the centuries. Today Dante bibliography is perhaps second to none. Yet obscure or controversial passages and unsolved riddles are still ordinary occurrences in the work. Every new book on Dante contains additional findings of some sort, or reveals a new and unsuspected dimension.

As the *Divine Comedy* was introduced into schools and assigned to young students for reading, the need for "study guides," "companions," "synopses," and other reading aides multiplied quickly. Each has a particular merit of its own, but the very fact that such didactic publications continue to appear proves that none of them seems to be fully satisfactory to all. Every study guide reflects a particular approach, a teaching methodology, the knowledge, the sensitivity and the individual interest of the preparer; it also reflects the particular exigencies of the times and the cultural trends of the reading public. These factors account for the proliferation of study guides that revise, update, and adapt their points of view to accommodate the cultural climate.

Under these circumstances new guides are always welcome and De Gennaro's endeavor deserves its own place among works of the kind. What distinguishes his *Companion* from previous works (often filled with dry facts, summaries, historical data, and references of all sorts) is precisely its departure from their conventional academic approach. His design is to outline Dante's entire journey by presenting a sequence of characters and episodes (the most relevant ones) that illuminate the poet's way from dark forest to vision of God. No display of erudition, no history, no minutiae, however interesting, but interpretation and narration, in which the warmth of his personal feeling is always present. Philological, historical, and philosophical problems are, in a sense, set aside, and the reading comes close to an esthetic experience, an attempt to re-live the feeling of the poet. Thus, Dante's intentions and achievements, his fervor and dis-

couragement, the drama of his mind and heart, are highligh-
ted by a restricted number of dominant figures that form a
continuum and that synthesize all the rest. The twenty-two
sections of the work round up the whole poem in a succinct,
well-balanced manner and convey not only the poet's lesson,
but also the highlights of his esthetic qualities.

For modern readers the main difficulty with the *Divine
Comedy* and similar works is their inability to translate the
material world into an image of the spiritual world, the
narrative of the journey into its moral meaning. The dominant realistic attitude of today's public does not easily allow
the mind to focus on more than one level of meaning at a
time. The idea of searching for underlying meanings, care-
fully hidden by a poet, is far removed from the habits of
modern students. This was not the case with medieval readers who were used to symbolism and evidently took pleasure
in digging for hidden allusions. It was believed that God,
who inspired the Bible, had expressed Himself in that
fashion, that is, by symbols.

Despite these difficulties, however, the reading of the
Divine Comedy is not only a fascinating experience, but also
a rewarding one. The poem is an image of our destiny. If it is
a compendium of the Middle Ages, which we call the "dark
age," it is not, however, a medieval work, but an eternal
one—eternal as are the problems that beset us in every age
and in every latitude. Dante cannot be confined to one city or
one nation alone, because, by virture of his poem, he has
become universal, belonging to all times and all nations. His
is the poem *by* Dante and *of* Dante; it is the man and the poet,
but it is also, and even more so, the poem of man, the account
of his perennial journey through the kingdom of evil, the
kingdom of expiation and redemption, and finally the kingdom of grace and salvation. Dante brings us from the material to the spiritual world; from earth to heaven; he uplifts
our spirit. Every step forward in the long and dramatic
journey is an advanced stage in the consciousness of our
state. Apart from the poetic delight, we seek in his poem an
escape from the "morta gora" of this world of suffering—a

new foundation for our knowledge, which modern science and technology cannot provide and have badly distorted. The great discoveries of science, however inebriating, have not been able to bury our metaphysical anguish; they have given us short-lived illusions. The anguish constantly returns with added vigor to torture our lives. No worldly science detached from divine wisdom can ever solve the essential problem of our existence. This was perhaps what Dante meant in his *Divine Comedy*.

Giovanni Gullace
S.U.N.Y. Binghamton

PREFACE

Dante Alighieri was born in Florence in the spring of 1265, and there he spent his childhood. He lost his mother when he was very young and his father remarried. He saw his city plunged into continuous civil wars. It was from Dante's memory of these wars that he called up an image of the river Arno "flowing less with water than with blood."[1]

Dante first met Beatrice in 1274 when he was nine; their second meeting took place nine years later. After Beatrice died in 1290, Dante wrote the *Vita Nuova* (*New Life*), a book that describes how, as a boy, he met a little girl of his own age and how he was in love with her from that hour to all eternity. Beatrice died young, but she became the inspiration for most of Dante's works and lived in his creative imagination to become, in the *Divine Comedy*, the guide to God himself.

Although in his young years Dante received an excellent education in classical and Christian literature, his immense intellectual curiosity impelled him to improve his education through his own efforts. In numerous passages of the *Divine Comedy* he reveals his familiarity with technical details of the most varied arts: architecture, sculpture, music, astronomy, etc. There is a touch of Leonardo or Alberti in Dante. Valuable friendships also assisted him in his own efforts. The poet Guido Cavalcanti guided Dante to the Sweet New Style* and may have stood beside him as he began to philosophize. Along with high aspirations and ideals, Brunetto Latini undoubtedly imparted to Dante grammar, rhetoric, and all sorts of practical knowledge. Possibly there were other influences such as the painter Giotto and the musician Casella. At the age of twenty-four Dante was a very learned man.

But at Florence, toward the end of the thirteenth century, it was impossible for a young man to live a life devoted to peace and scholarly study. If not by choice, then by force of circumstances, Dante was caught up in the flow of events. He belonged to the Bianchi (the Whites), one of the rival factions within the Guelf party, and after the Neri (the Blacks) took power late in 1301, Dante and others were exiled (1302).

Dante lived henceforward as an outcast, always troubled by the "bitter taste of another's bread, the hard road of another's stair," and so it was to be for the remaining twenty years of his life. It is true that Dante's exile contributed to the artistic quality of the *Divine Comedy*, without which Dante's work would lack that intensity of feeling which is often the source of poetry. It would also have been deprived of that understanding of the human heart which is the result of the contact with peoples of different temperament and customs. Nevertheless, the exile caused him the most bitter suffering—he became a "displaced person."

During his exile Dante traveled to Verona, Lucca and

*Sweet New Style: instead of the stress on frank sensuality found in the Provençal poets, the poets of the Sweet New Style preferred to love women as embodiments of pure or abstract beauty.

even, perhaps, to Paris, and eventually settled in Ravenna under the protection of its ruler, Guido da Polenta. But the sufferings of the exile had taken their toll. Boccaccio tells us that, as his literary work became known, "people who saw his tragic and somber form go by would say to one another: 'There is a man who has been to hell and back again'."[2]

This sadness was also the result of other factors. Dante had been deprived of the joys of family life. His wife, Gemma Donati, whom he had married perhaps in 1292, and his two sons and one or two daughters had not accompanied him into exile. Dante had been saddened by the policies of the French king, Philip IV, which had led to the humiliation of Pope Boniface VIII in the outrage of Anagni. (At Anagni in 1303, the pope was made a prisoner and was probably physically mistreated by the followers of Philip IV.) Dante had hoped to see the reunion of Italy and Germany under Emperor Henry VII, but his hopes had ended with the latter's death in 1313.

Dante died in Ravenna on September 14, 1321, and he is buried there. There he lies, close to the Church of St. Francis where he often went to pray and meditate.

Dante wrote the *Divine Comedy* during the last years of his life. The poem has 100 cantos. After one introductory canto, the remaining 99 are divided into three parts (*Inferno*, *Purgatorio*, *Paradiso*) of 33 cantos each. It is one of three or four priceless jewels in Europe's literary crown.

It is in many ways a difficult work, containing the narration of innumerable events, an immense erudition in philosophy and theology, as well as a great knowledge of astronomy, painting and music. Finally, it is a difficult work because of Dante's constant use of allegory that is often obscure—allegory that has baffled scholars across the centuries.

The fact remains, however, that in spite of its difficulty and immense erudition, the *Divine Comedy* is a unique artistic achievement. The beauty of language, the unfailing execution in every detail and, above all, the grandeur of the poet's vision have given mankind a new idea of the power of genius.

The grandeur of this vision ranges from the descriptions of Dante's journey through Hell, Purgatory and Heaven to the representation of the numerous personages he meets on the road; from emphasis on resplendent images to stress on nightmare visions; from political, social and religious views to a Christian spirit thirsty for a world of beauty, truth and justice.

The historical framework within which this grandeur of vision takes place is not more than the first two decades of the fourteenth century. Every other historical age appears as a casual reminiscence, and every recollection of previous events and historical ages is only episodic, illustrative or decorative. Dante hardly mentions the Crusades, the great popes from Leo I to Innocent IV, and great representatives of the struggle between the papacy and the empire, such as Gregory VII and Henry IV, are absent.

Dante concentrates on the Florence, the papacy and the Holy Roman Empire of the fourteenth century.[3] The battles of Montaperti, Campaldino, the civil wars between the Bianchi and the Neri, the figures of Farinata, Brunetto Latini, Cacciaguida are part of the history of Florence. The figures of Justinian, Manfred, Henry VII, Boniface VIII and Clement V are men who played an important part in the history of the empire or the papacy. Dante was very anxious about the fate of Florence and the empire, an anxiety that was outweighed only by his anxiety for the Church, and it led him to concentrate his attention on the Church as supernatural guide of that society and keystone of its existence. No literary work has ever been so concerned about the role of the Church as has the *Divine Comedy*. For Dante the Church was to be pure, faithful to the precepts of Christ, free from corruption and impurity. For Dante the Church, which was the Bride of Christ, the repository of truth, the sacred institution "suckled" on the blood of Peter, Linus and Cletus, was to be a spiritual and not a temporal power. Dante feels and lives this view deeply. One hundred times or more he breaks off his narrative to utter the cry of hate and contempt which rises in his throat: the cry against the corrupt clergy.

Thus the *Divine Comedy*, besides being a great work of art, is also a work that gives utterance in immortal language to the sublimity of the Christian ideal. Though this ideal was often betrayed by the representatives of the Church, Dante felt the need to restore the Christian ideal in order to bring peace and harmony to the chaotic world.

Angelo A. De Gennaro
Los Angeles, California

INFERNO

CHAPTER I

INTRODUCTION.

Midway in our life's journey, I went astray
from the straight road and woke to find myself
alone in a darkwood.

In the spring of the year of 1300, with these famous words, the thirty-five year old Dante Alighieri starts his journey from the dark wood to the Hereafter. The journey begins on April 8 and ends on April 15.

According to medieval tradition, spring is the time when God created the world and, therefore, the "sweet season" is a good omen for Dante's journey. As God created the world in the spring, so Dante attempted to create his new spiritual life during the same season. The mixture of literal and allegorical meaning—which is one of the main traits of the *Divine Comedy*—is evident here. The mixture may be somewhat ambiguous and, to the reader unschooled in the Christian tradition, confusing. It does, however, enrich the poem with intellectual power.

The year is 1300. It is the memorable year when Pope Boniface VIII proclaimed the Jubilee for the first time in the history of the Church. The indulgences issued by the Pope were put forth to aid troubled souls and to hasten and facilitate the entrance to Heaven of the poor souls in Purgatory.

The idea of the journey to the Hereafter was familiar to people of the Middle Ages. Many ancient authors, for example, Homer and Virgil, had pictured the living visiting the dead. There were Moslem poems describing journeys to Heaven and Hell. It is also known that Celtic monks, in the feverish solitude of their convents, had written many such tales around the persons of St. Brendan or St. Patrick. But upon this common ground, Dante erected a monumental structure, a structure combining his personal and historical experiences with the eternal realities of the Middle Ages.

The idea of the dark wood as a symbol of sin was also familiar to the Middle Ages. We find it, for example, in Joachim da Fiore's writings. But Dante transforms the allegorical image of the dark wood into a real one.

> Death could scarce be more bitter than that place!
> . . .
> How I came to it I cannot rightly say
> so drugged and loose with sleep had I become
> . . .
> Just as a swimmer, who with his last breath
> . . .
> flounders ashore from perilous seas, might turn
> to memorize the wide waters of his death—
>
> so did I turn, my soul still fugitive
> from death's surviving image. . . .

The wood ceases to be the symbol of sin and becomes the place where we witness the drama of a soul in pain.

The wood is "dreary," "rank," "wild," and though Dante suffers from its horrors, he can see the "dilettoso colle," "the delightful hill" of virtue. Three beasts block his way; the leopard, the lion and the she-wolf. They symbolize lust, pride and avarice, the earthly passions that Dante is not able to control.

Dante is in difficulty, but Heaven, moved by Beatrice's love, intervenes to save him. Thus when the poet is being driven back by the she-wolf into the wood and he almost despairs, the shade of Virgil appears to him.

At first Dante is amazed but, upon recognizing the poet and author whom he venerates, he expresses his admiration for him.

> "And are you then that Virgil and that fountain of
> purest speech? . . .
>
> For you are my true master and first author,
> the sole maker from whom I drew the breath
> of that sweet style whose measures have brought me
> honor."   I

Dante greatly admires Virgil's harmonious, clear style, which had influenced his own manner of expression. Dante's writing developed from the still childish *Vita Nuova*, with its mystical playing with the symbolism of numbers, into a mature style. But we also sense that Virgil, who had been dead for thirteen centuries when he meets Dante in the wood, goes on living within Dante, providing him with good company.

For most of his life, Dante chose Virgil for company. He chose him over Homer, perceiving in Virgil a world closer to Christianity in the choice, order and relationship of its values. There is in Virgil a spiritual vastness that embraces everything from the blade of grass to the stars; there is a feeling of love for everything that is not evil; there is an aspiration toward a world of beauty, goodness and justice. The dream of Virgil is a society, in the words of Concetto Marchesi, "of compassionate men who work in peace on the fertile earth blessed by heaven."[1]

For Dante poetry and wisdom are inseparable. (This is true, I believe, in poets of the highest rank, from Dante himself to Shakespeare and Goethe.) Thus Virgil, the great poet, becomes the symbol of true wisdom in the *Divine Comedy*.

What is wisdom? For Joseph Pieper wisdom is the realization of the good, and the realization of the good presupposes knowledge of reality. "He alone can do good who knows what things are like and what their situation is. The preeminence of wisdom means that so-called 'good intentions' and so-called 'meaning well' by no means suffice. Realization of the good presupposes that our actions are appropriate to the real situation, that is to the concrete realities which form the 'environment' of a concrete human action; and that we therefore take this concrete reality seriously, with clear-eyed objectivity."[2] In some men this wisdom may appear fitfully or, to quote T.S. Eliot, "once in a lifetime, in the rapture of a single experience, beautific or awful."[3] In Virgil it appears constant, steady and serene.

But Virgil, besides being a symbol of true wisdom, is also characterized by a lofty and exquisite humanity. He is not the scholastic or academic teacher, but he is now tender, now considerate, and especially in the *Purgatorio*, "he is ineffably melancholic"[4] due to his awareness that this world does not constitute salvation for him. The passions and feelings of the man break out from under his stoic appearance.

Virgil is a poet, a sage and a man of profound humanity and, therefore, we are not at all surprised when Dante takes him as his guide through Hell and Purgatory.

CHAPTER II

BEATRICE. THE VESTIBULE OF HELL. LIMBO.

Beatrice's love for Dante has not had to endure the wear and tear of life, the merciless erosion caused by habit and daily contact. It is this love that constitutes the main theme of the *Divine Comedy*.

It is this love that is behind the action of Beatrice. She descends into the Limbo of Hell, where Virgil is, and beseeches him to go to the aid of Dante, who finds himself in distress in the dark wood.

Both the scene and the character of Beatrice are without precedent. She speaks the language of earthly love: "Love is what moves me." She is in pain because her beloved Dante is in mortal danger: "She spoke and turned away to hide a tear."   II

Dante reciprocates Beatrice's love, and he expresses it in beautiful verses.

> Her eyes were kindled from the lamps of Heaven.
> Her voice reached through me, tender, sweet, and low.
> An angel's voice, a music of its own.
>
> II

Beatrice's eyes and voice, to quote Francesco Flora, "illuminate and soften the harshest verses of the *Comedy* and they enhance the quality of the most beautiful ones."[1]

Dante's love for Beatrice becomes sublimated and she, the woman, becomes the guide to the "Primo Amore," "the Prime Love," the God who sometimes reveals Himself to mortals in mystical contemplation, in the lightening flash of genius, or in the overwhelming sweetness of a spring morning.

Dante and Beatrice love each other, but it is her love for him that is the real cause of the action. It is Beatrice who gives Virgil full power to guide Dante through Hell and Purgatory so that Dante, in seeing the effects of sin, may be led toward the path of salvation; so that Dante may discover the way of light by climbing the painful mountain of Purgatory.

Before Virgil and Dante set out on their memorable journey, Dante compares himself critically with Aeneas and Paul who had also journeyed to the Hereafter. Dante is a mere man among men, only a baffled soul, "why should he go there, and who grants it?" Virgil tells Dante that the Virgin Mary, St. Lucia and Beatrice care for him in the court of Heaven, protecting him in the fearful enterprise. Dante's spirits rise in joyous anticipation. He will follow Virgil through Hell and Purgatory. Dante expresses this feeling with a delicate simile:

> As flowerlets drooped and puckered in the night
> turn up to the returning sun and spread
> their petals wide on his new warmth and light—
>
> just so my wilted spirits rose again. . .
>
> II

This simile is perfection. The love of the three ladies becomes the returning sun, and the rise of Dante's spirits becomes the flowers standing all open on their stems.

Thus Dante and Virgil start the sorrowful and painful journey through Hell, the first region of the Hereafter.

Hell is the painful world of evil done on our earth, the evil caused by uncontrollable instincts, by wicked behavior. The law of symbolic retribution makes the punishment fit the crime. The punishment is carried out now by natural elements such as furious rain, howling wind, raining fire, stench, darkness, biting cold, now by demons who are capricious, malicious, spiteful and cruel. Both terror and pain are depicted by vivid verses:

> Here sighs and cries and wails coiled and recoiled
> on the starless air, spilling my soul to tears.
>
> III

Dante's view of Hell is creative as is his view of its Vestibule. He places in it the souls who are worthy neither of Hell nor Paradise, because in life they were neither good nor evil. They were souls who passed through life indifferent, worthless, leaving no trace behind. With them are the feeble angels who, when Lucifer rebelled, drew aside in cowardice and held neither for God nor for Lucifer. They are also the marked egoists, too bad for Heaven, too decent for Hell.

These souls preferred inertia to an active life and Dante, under the influence of Aristotle, who views virtue as activity, punishes them. The image of their punishment is the opposite of their inertia. These wretches "who were never alive" eternally pursue an elusive, ever-shifting banner, and they are goaded by swarms of wasps and hornets. Virgil will say: "Let us not speak to them, look and pass on." What could Virgil and Dante say to these souls who never had any ideals, good or bad, who never took any stand on the issues of life? Dante recognizes several souls, among them Pope Celestine V "who in cowardice made the Great Denial." The Pope is punished because, by renouncing the papacy, he shirked personal responsibility.   III

Dante punishes these inert souls because for him virtue, or the realization of humanity, was activity. There may be another reason. Dante, for whom principles were incarnate beings and errors had the faces of men, could not really side with inert souls. Dante, who had a passionate temperament and an unyielding determination, could not sympathize with people who were not active in life. Dante, who could not stand apart when truth was at stake, could not be indifferent to people who lived "senza infamia e senza lode," "without infamy and without praise."   III

Dante and Virgil move on toward the river Acheron, the first of the rivers of Hell. The recently dead souls of the damned fall on its banks, like leaves in autumn, and the monstrous Charon, who "wears a wheel of flame around each eye," ferries them across the river to punishment.

A livid light envelops, to quote Francesco Flora, "this lugubrious infernal autumn,"[2] and the monstrous steerman bellows:

> ". . .Woe to you depraved souls! Bury
>
> here and forever all hope of Paradise:
> I come to lead you to the other shore,
> into eternal dark, into fire and ice."

                                                        III

On hearing these harsh words, the souls begin to blaspheme "...God, their parents, their time on earth,/the race of Adam, and the day and the hour/and the place and the seed and the womb that gave/them birth."

It is a description that carries us right to the edge of the abyss, for here horror is added to horror, to make it the greatest monument of human despair in the world of literature. Among those influenced by this scene was Michelangelo in his *Last Judgment*. Like Dante, he depicts a terrible world in the terrifying chaos of his masterpiece on the wall of the Sistine Chapel, a world full of hatred, cruelty and suffering. It could not have been otherwise. Both men were torn between their desire to exalt the power of the human spirit and their realization of the tragedy inherent in the drama of the human soul.

Dante and Virgil reach the first circle of Limbo, the place, according to the Church Fathers, of the unbaptized children. To this orthodox doctrine Dante makes a bold addition. He includes the virtuous pagans who did not know the true God but who promoted the nobility of the human spirit in themselves and human civilization. In Dante's Limbo we find Plato, Caesar and Averroes. These souls are not tormented, but they sigh because they have no hope of seeing God: "...sounds of sighing rose from every side,/sending a tremor through the timeless air."   IV

Here, moving away from the narrow, orthodox outlook, Dante pays homage to human greatness of all ages. He glorifies human genius.

CHAPTER III

HELL. FRANCESCA AND PAOLO. CIACCO.

Hell, which Dante imagines as a great funnel-shaped cave lying below the northern hemisphere, consists of nine circles. The eighth circle is scored by ten indentations, forming a series of ditches called *Malebolge* (dirty ditches). The ninth circle is a well.

Hell is an abyss, the "abysmal valley," the dark region, the starless air, the place of the "souls who have lost the good of the intellect," the place where the tumult of hoarse, shrill voices roar like seas wracked by a war of winds, the place of demoniac cruelty and terrible suffering.

Dante and Virgil slowly become accustomed to the darkness of Hell, and they are able to see the landscape: enormous stones, steep places, cliffs, hewed rocks, dark slopes, sandy, barren lands, wild paths, ditches, caves, difficult pathways, a tragic wood, a river of blood, fires, a frozen lake, and eternal, cursed rains of fire and water.

The description of the landscape is so extraordinarily precise that it is possible to draw maps and plans and to build models of that country beyond the grave. But across the landscape a perpetual shifting of figures, episodes, and allusions transforms Hell into a dreamland forest where powerful images succeed nightmare visions, a universe "so wonderful," says Daniel-Rops, "that it is hard to know how any man could have conceived it."[1]

Hell really begins with the second circle. Here, blocking the way, sits Minos, the dread monster who judges the damned and assigns to each soul its eternal torment in a particular circle, which he designates with the number of times he girds himself with his tail.

The setting of the second circle is the whirlwind, which sweeps and beats the carnal sinners: Semiramis, Dido, Cleopatra, Helen, Achilles, Paris, Tristan, Paolo and Francesca. Dante punishes them, but he also makes use of delicate images to show sympathy toward them: "As the wings of wintering starlings bear them on. . ." "As cranes go over sounding their harsh cry. . ." "As mating doves that love calls to their nest. . . ."   V

Dante shows both severity and compassion, especially when he portrays the figures of Paolo and Francesca, who are driven by the wind together, and who will never be separated because death caught them sinning together. Francesca is an adulteress but she is marked by kindliness. She does not curse God but wishes that God were her friend. Francesca is a sinner but she is also delicate. Paolo "breathed on my lips the tremor of his kiss." Francesca is a reprobate but she is also lyrical, intensely effusive: "Love, which in gentlest hearts will soonest bloom." Francesca is a sinner but also a victim. Love is not the product of our free determination; it is a natural force that comes outside of us and seizes us: "Love, which permits no loved one not to love,/ took me so strongly with delight in him. . . ."   V

This is the quality that makes Dante one of the greatest moral forces of the world. He is a severe judge and a compassionate man. Shelley states: "A man to be greatly good must imagine intensely and comprehensively. . .the pains and pleasures of his species must become his own."[2] Dante is as "greatly good" as Shelley suggests. Dante condemns Francesca and Paolo, begging us all the time for pity and compassion. Among the poets no one but Shakespeare can touch Dante here.

But there is more than compassion and severity in Dante. There is the great creation of the character of Francesca for whom love is not a poet's dream but a piece of real life rooted deep in the crude common soil of humanity—a piece of reality that is physical attraction, but also "desiato riso" ("longed-for smile"), trembling lips, as well as the time "del costui piacer sì forte" (the time of "delight"), the time in which our imagination abolishes all distance and creates a world in which there lives only the person we love. Here Dante re-echoes the sensuality of Courtly Love and the spirituality of the Sweet New Style.

I believe Dante's creation of the character of Francesca also reflects Dante's own feeling and inner spiritual experience. Some artists have been able to keep their lives and their creations in different compartments. Dante does not. His reaction to Francesca's tale ("Francesca, what you suffer here / melts me to tears of pity and of pain") illuminates the delicate, exquisite side of his personality.

Dante is so stricken by compassion for the tragic fate of Francesca and Paolo that he swoons. He recovers from this swoon and finds himself in the third circle where the gluttons are punished. Cerberus, the ravenous three-headed dog of Hell, personifies the sin of gluttony. The souls lie on the ground under rain that is "eternal, cursed, cold and charged with woe," and the monstrous Cerberus, with his hands "armed with claws," "graffia gli spiriti, scuoia ed isquadra" ("rips the wretches, flays and mangles them").

In this scene, Dante exercises his visual and aural powers—powers that were never withered by his book-learning and vast erudition. Here Dante forces us to be there, watching the horrid scene. The words themselves are onomatopoetic. With "scuoia ed isquadra," the reader *hears* the ripping and mangling of bodies.

As Dante and Virgil pass, one of the souls sits up and addresses Dante. He is Ciacco, the Hog, a parasite and a glutton, a citizen of Dante's own Florence.

The figure of Ciacco is connected with the Florentine political events, which take the form of prophecy. By a curious law, the souls in Hell have knowledge of both past and future events, so that Ciacco is able to inform Dante of events in Florence later than Easter of 1300, the fictitious date of the poem. In the year 1302, the citizens of Dante's divided Florence will come to a showdown in which the Blacks will seize power and the Whites, including Dante, will be exiled.

The figure of Ciacco is imbued with the love for the "dolce mondo," for our wonderful terrestrial world, a love that Ciacco reveals to Dante in moving tones: "But when you move again among the living, / oh, speak my name to the memory of men!" For the damned souls the real world, the world to which, to quote Francesco Flora, "they turn their affection which Heaven rejects,"[3] is still our earth. Our earth is a living reality to these souls, a sensual passion, a collection of emotional attachments.   VI

CHAPTER IV

THE HOARDERS. FILIPPO ARGENTI. FARINATA.

As the poets enter the fourth circle, the monster Plutus menaces them. Dante and Virgil later encounter two raging mobs. One mob is made up of the hoarders, the other of the wasters. The two mobs meet, clash against each other and exchange insults. The hoarders shout: "Why do you waste?" The wasters shout: "Why do you hoard?" Dante is so contemptuous of these sinners that he portrays no soul in this circle. He ridicules them.

"Master," I said, "what people can these be?
And all those tonsured ones there on our left—
is it possible they *all* were of the clergy?"

VII

Dante despises these souls because he judges them in the light of his Christian ethics. If a waster is a soul who has not made good use of his personal wealth, a hoarder is a soul who, in his insatiable desire for wealth, possesses neither a seed of generosity, nor the faculty of self-surrender, nor an openness of heart. The hoarder, with his totally economic view of life and intense devotion to calculation, is a soul closed to love and grace.

The theme of Dante's Fortune arises here. In medieval mythology she was the goddess, often represented as a female figure holding an ever-revolving wheel, who unpredictably determines events or issues favorably or unfavorably. Dante incorporates her in his scheme of the universe and ranks her among the angels. She becomes the minister of change, and though men blaspheme her name, "she in her beatitude does not hear." Disappointed, outcast, impoverished, Dante had much to tempt him to cynical views, yet he identifies Fortune with Divine Providence.   VII

The poets come to a black spring, which bubbles murkily over the rocks to form the marsh of Styx. It is the fifth circle where the souls of the wrathful are punished. They lie in the marsh and attack each other. "They bit / as if each would tear the other limb from limb." Some of them, the souls of the sullen, lie entombed in the slime and gurgle in their throats a dismal chant. Even these souls sigh for the terrestrial world, for the "air made sweet by the sun."   VII

The poets come to the foot of a high tower. Before reaching it, they observe two flame signals rise from its summit, and another make answer at a great distance. The poets see before them a broad marsh and the demon Phlegias coming with angry rapidity to ferry them over it. Phlegias believes that Dante is a damned soul, but he is mistaken. Phlegias will only ferry the two poets across the broad marsh, or fifth circle.

It is during the crossing of the marsh that Dante, interpreting his own law of symbolic retribution in a strange way, gives us an example of his anger. A spirit, all covered with mud, addresses Dante, and Dante recognizes him. It is Filippo Argenti of the old Adimari family, noted for his ostentation and brutal anger. He was also a personal enemy of Dante. His old hatred toward Argenti still quivers in him. " 'May you weep and wail to all eternity, / for I know you, hell-dog, filthy as you are.' " Dante has himself praised by Virgil with an intemperate apostrophe. " 'Indignant spirit, I kiss you as you frown. / Blessed be she who bore you.' " Dante gloats at seeing the other sinners fall upon Argenti and rip him to pieces, and Dante, in recalling the scene while he is writing, praises and thanks God for it.   VIII

The episode is very dramatic, and it shows another side of Dante, his vindictive spirit. The human demon who delights in contemplating the writhings of a tortured spirit is a part of the poet himself. This vindictiveness is our security. It assures us that Dante is not afraid to reveal his true nature. Nothing but the truth, the whole appalling truth about himself will satisfy him, a necessary condition for the creation of great poetry.

The boat meanwhile speeds on, and before the poets disembark, a new setting appears. Before them lie the flaming red towers of the city of Dis, the capital of Hell—a setting inhabited by terrifying creatures. The demons refuse to let the poets pass, and the three infernal Furies, who have the parts and bearing of women and are girded with hydras of bright green, threaten and call for Medusa to come and change Dante into stone. It is a frightening scene—one that makes us relive our bad dreams.

This setting sheds further light on Dante's personality and completes our image of him. If there is delicacy of feeling in Francesca, love-hate for Florence in Ciacco, anger in Argenti, there is also the ability to vividly portray the horrendous ugliness of the Furies.

Dante waits in dread, but his anxiety dissolves at the appearance of the heavenly messenger. Divine omnipotence triumphs over diabolic insolence. Dante expresses this victorious mood with three tercets, which have a pressing beat:

Suddenly there broke on the dirty swell
of the dark marsh a squall of terrible sound
that sent a tremor through both shores of Hell;

a sound as if two continents of air,
one frigid and one scorching, clashed head on
in a war of winds that stripped the forests bare,

ripped off whole boughs and blew them helter skelter
along the range of dust it raised before it
making the beasts and shepherds run for shelter.

IX

The heavenly messenger has arrived and with a touch
throws open the gate of Dis. The damned souls scatter before
the one "who crossed dry-shod / the Stygian marsh into
Hell's burning bowels;" and the poets, unopposed, find
themselves in the sixth circle.

Here the poets find a countryside that resembles a vast
cemetery. Dante and Virgil observe everywhere fiery tombs
with their lids open. Cries of pain issue endlessly from these
entombed dead. Dante seems to have seized upon our nightmare visions and imprisoned them in this scene.

Among these souls, those who denied the immortality of
the soul is Farinata degli Uberti, the leader of the Ghibelline
party in Florence. Dante, however, does not mention Farinata's heresy. Instead he portrays Farinata's patriotic spirit,
stressing his great love for Florence. The members of Farinata's party, driven by hatred against the Florentine Guelfs,
wanted to raze Florence after the battle of Montaperti, but it
was Farinata who saved her. "But I *was* alone at that time
when every other / consented to the death of Florence; I /
alone with open face defended her." Farinata loves Florence
more than he hates his Florentine enemies.

Farinata, whose love for Florence was the main concern of
his life, becomes a powerful figure in the hands of Dante:
"Erect, he rose above the flame, great chest, great brow; / he
seemed to hold all Hell in disrespect." Dante has a sense of

power. The same power is expressed in the gigantic nudes of Michelangelo and Tintoretto. It is expressed by Dante in the creation of Farinata's character, his towering figure and his scorn of the flames of Hell. Hell itself seems diminished before this mighty soul.   X

Here Dante introduces the delicate and profound theme of paternal love. Cavalcante Cavalcanti is the father of Guido, who was "the first among Dante's friends" and a poet of distinction. Cavalcante, in hearing Dante speaking to Farinata, rises from the tomb and asks Dante why Guido is not with him. Cavalcante mistakenly infers from Dante's reply that Guido is dead and he swoons back into the flames. And all this with words so infused with life that we are compelled to grant the reality of the scene. The scene is depicted with only seven tercets; nevertheless, how well Dante communicates its poignancy!

Cavalcante's touching scene has not affected Farinata, who is too self-absorbed to notice it. He has other preoccupations. What torments him more than his "flaming bed" is the thought that the members of his family are by repeated decrees expressly denied permission to return to Florence:

> ". . .why is that populace so savage
> in the edicts they pronounce against my strain?"

                                                        X

Dante understands the torment of Farinata. Future events, as Farinata prophesies, will also tear Dante from an easygoing existence in Florence, devoted to literature, and will expose him to the vicissitudes of a wandering life. The theme of exile in Ciacco returns.

The figure of Farinata has fascinated Dante's readers for generations. Dante has portrayed all the degradations of human nature. He has depicted the ignoble side of man, and to this interest he has added a world of beauty and force, a vision of noble humanity. Dante initiated what Michelangelo will complete, the depiction of the type of man best suited to ennoble the earth.

CHAPTER V

THE DIVISION OF HELL. PIER DELLA VIGNA.

Before Dante and Virgil come to the seventh circle, Virgil, under the influence of Aristotle, who classifies sins under the headings of vice, incontinence, and bestiality, outlines in detail the geography of Hell. Incontinence is punished outside the city of Dis; violence, bestiality, fraud and malice are punished within it.

The poets now begin descending the fallen rock wall, and they come to the seventh circle, which is the circle of the violent. They behold the Minotaur, the offspring of Minos, the king of Crete, and of Parsiphaë. The Minotaur menaces the poets, but Virgil tricks him and they hurry by.

41

The seventh circle is divided into three rounds forming a landscape of livid waters, bare trees and arid sand.

The river of blood, the Phlegethon, marks the first round to which are consigned for punishment those who have done violence against their neighbors, the great war-makers, the cruel tyrants, highwaymen, from Alexander the Great to Attila the Scourge of God.

The banks of the river Phlegethon are patroled by the Centaurs, who are ready to shoot with arrows any sinner who raises himself out of the boiling blood beyond the limits permitted him. Dante's creative imagination takes the Centaurs' "riding as once on earth they rode to the chase" from mythology and makes them the protagonists of a newer and crueler hunt, the hunting of men.   XII

In the dark light, surrounded by the river of blood, appears the wood of suicides where souls are encased in thorny trees.

Dante compares the wood with our natural world. "Its foliage was not verdant, but nearly black. / The unhealthy branches, gnarled and warped and tangled, / bore poison thorns instead of fruit." The comparison makes the wood, says Francesco Flora, "more sinister,"[1] and our imagination, alive amid the contrasts of the simile, goes wild with emotion and amazement.   XIII

Dante accentuates the sinister quality of the wood by making it funereal. On Judgment Day the suicides will go for their bodies, but they will not be able to reinhabit them; the bodies will dangle from the trees until the end of time.

The odious Harpies have their nest here, and Dante portrays them vividly. "Their wings are wide, their feet clawed, their huge bellies / covered with feathers, their necks and faces human. / They croak eternally in the unnatural trees."   XIII

A subdued lament and weeping swells and quivers through the wood; no human creature can be seen. It seems as if someone were hidden behind the thicket. Dante, shuddering, stops. But when at Virgil's bidding, he breaks off a twig from a tree, the tree cries out in human tones and begs for mercy. "As a green branch with one end all aflame / will hiss and sputter sap out of the other / as the air escapes—so from that trunk there came / words and blood together, gout by gout." Dante's simile, which echoes a simile of Virgil's, introduces a very tragic story.   XIII

It is the story of the Chancellor Pier della Vigna who, being accused of high treason against his master, the Hohenstaufen Frederick II, killed himself, and "though just" he became "unjust" to himself. Now he states and swears that he was loyal to his master. "I was so faithful to my glorious office / that for it I gave up both sleep and life." And he asks Dante "to vindicate in the memory of men / one who lies prostrate from the blows of Envy."   XIII

Dante shows a great sympathy toward Pier della Vigna because of his nobility of character, but also because Dante saw that Pier experienced something much like his own subjective reality. The world of the *Divine Comedy* is full of characters who speak for themselves but also of characters in whom their creator is always present. In the case of Pier della Vigna, the similarities between the creator and the created are striking. Pier della Vigna was a poet, an administrator, a true defender of lay authority against the arrogant pretensions of the Church, and he was unjustly accused by the king's courtiers. Dante saw in him the story of his own life.

Suddenly, the poets see two souls being pursued by a pack of savage hounds. The hounds overtake one of the souls who had sought refuge behind a bush. They tear him to pieces, and go off carrying his limbs in their teeth. Even the soul who is encased in the bush suffers from the hounds' rage as they tear at the bush. It is the soul of a Florentine. Dante, driven by the love for his native land, gathers the scattered leaves and restores them to the doleful shade.

The scene, which shows both Dante's power as a writer and his humanity as a man, is very frightening. The bloodthirsty hounds, the cries of the souls, the darkness that envelops the sinister landscape, the distance from the earth—all these things create a fearful, eerie world.

The river Phlegethon surrounds the wood which, in turn,

encircles the third round of the seventh circle, a thick and arid land upon which descends an eternal, slow rain of fire. "[G]reat flakes of flame fell slowly / as snow falls in the Alps on a windless day."   XIV

Here, on the sand, are three classes of sinners scorched and weakened by the rain of fire: the blasphemers stretched supine on the ground, the sodomites running in endless circles, and the usurers huddled on the sand.

But the fire does not weaken or intimidate Capaneus who continues to blaspheme and scorn the fire. The man, who had challenged the gods and who had been struck by Jove's lightning, still continues to defy him. "What I was living, the same am I now, dead."   XIV

One more sinister landscape: the river Phlegethon flows out of the wood, and its bed and banks are made of stones. Its vapors extinguish the rain of fire.

To explain the source of the infernal rivers, Virgil discourses on how they spring from the statue of the Old Man of Crete. His tears originate the rivers Acheron, Styx, Phlegethon, and Cocytus at the bottom of Hell, as well as the river Lethe, which flows in the Terrestrial Paradise.

The story starts with a faraway tone which creates a world of mystery. "In the middle of the sea, and gone to waste, / there lies a country known as Crete,. . . An ancient giant stands in the mountain's core." A less remote tone could only have assimilated the world of the Old Man to the landscapes of the earth with which we are familiar. As it is, the impression of the world of the Old Man of Crete that we retain is the most suitable one, the impression of a remote world that attracts and excites us.   XIV

CHAPTER VI

BRUNETTO LATINI. GERYON.
SEDUCERS.

As Dante walks along the banks of the river Phlegethon where the sodomites, the violent against nature, are punished, one of the sinners stops him. With great difficulty the poet recognizes him under his baked features as Ser Brunetto Latini, who had been his teacher and friend.

Dante's great interest in, and understanding of, individual human beings is the result of a very affectionate observation of men and women. This habit—this gift is lavished on the character of Brunetto to create his reality and his nobility. He is the man of much experience who cheered Dante and encouraged his talents in his adolescence. In his

45

writings, he is the great interpreter of the wisdom of Rome, and he taught Dante "how man makes himself eternal." He is the man of high rank in the city's government who, had he lived, would have defended the just Dante against the unjust Florentine people. Here again is a return of the theme of exile, which we have already seen in Ciacco and Farinata.

If Brunetto's character is real, the character of Dante is also real. Dante is filled with intense feeling, which he must express to obtain relief. He speaks of his love, mixed with pity and agony, toward his friend and teacher Brunetto:

> "For that sweet image, gentle and paternal,
> you were to me in the world when hour by hour
> you taught me how man makes himself eternal,
>
> lives in my mind, and now strikes to my heart."

XV

It seems to me that, whenever an author creates a particularly vital character, there is always something of himself there—some trait of his own, some strength or weakness, some aspiration, some desire, some emotion of his own. In the character of his teacher and friend Brunetto, Dante, whose parents died when he was very young, has put his hunger for paternal affection.

Among the sodomites the poets find notable warriors, statesmen, knights and magnates such as Guido Guerra, Tagliaio Aldobrandi, Jacopo Resticucci. They ask Dante for news of Florence, and he replies with a passionate lament for her present degradation:

> "O Florence! your sudden wealth and your upstart
> rabble, dissolute and overweening,
> already set you weeping in your heart!"

XVI

We see how the poet, since his meeting with Brunetto, slowly and gradually builds himself a seat of judgment, from which height he flings his curt judgment of the Florentine bourgeoisie. If medieval doctrine found the root of all evil in the sin of pride, Dante finds it in the sin of cupidity. If pride seems to be the sin of the feudal and hierarchical age, "i subiti guadagni," or greed seems to be the sin of the rising bourgeoisie in Dante's world.

Further on, on the utmost limit of the seventh circle, the usurers are seated near the cliff. They are sitting in a crouch with tears gushing from their eyes, warding off the flames with their hands, and each of them has a purse blazoned with a coat of arms, hanging from his neck. Dante recognizes none of them but their coats of arms unmistakably belong to famous Florentine families.

It is easy to see why Dante punishes the usurers with fire. For Dante usury, to quote John Sinclair, is "a kind of blasphemy to be punished by fire"[1] because the usurer does not earn money with the sweat of his brow: "By this, recalling the Old Testament / near the beginning of Genesis, you will see / that in the will of Providence, man was meant to labor and to prosper." We also find Dante's criticism in St. Thomas and the early Fathers of the Church.

The theme of the flight over the abyss starts here. Dante's verses express the joy and wonder of someone who has been granted his most heartfelt wish, to see his imaginings become a living reality.

At Virgil's command Dante removes a cord from around his waist, and Virgil drops it over the edge of the abyss. As if in answer to a signal, the monstrous figure of Geryon, who has a human face and a snakelike body and who is the ugly symbol of fraud, comes swimming through the dirty air of the pit and lands on the stoney brink. The monster shows only his head and face.

The description of the flight of Geryon, with the poets on his back, shows Dante's poetic visual power. He is able to give the reader a sense of particularity, to make us see a particular being in a particular place and time. Geryon:

> swung about, and stretching out his tail
> he worked it like an eel, and with his paws
> he gathered in the air, while I turned pale.
> . . .
> slowly, he swims on through space,
> wheels and descends,
> . . .
> And once freed of our weight, he shot from there
> . . .
> into the dark like an arrow into air.
>
> XVII

Dante's sense of particularity or visual capacity is so intense and clear that we *see* and we *believe*.

Geryon deposits the poets at the foot of the great cliff in the eighth circle, "a lost place of stone / as black as the great cliff that seals it round." As various moats encircle ancient castles, ten concentric ditches (*bolge*) score this eighth circle, at the bottom of which lies the well of the giants and Satan, the ninth and final circle of Hell. To pass from one ditch (*bolgia*) to another, one must cross on stone dikes that serve as bridges.   XVIII

What makes the eighth circle interesting is first, the story of Dante's and Virgil's journey through the dark and cruel regions of Hell, and second, Dante's skill in varying the story to avoid monotony. Before our eyes parade all kinds of human vices, from the seducers to the flatterers, from the simoniacs to the fortune tellers, from the thieves to the sowers of discord.

Contributing to the great variety of the story is the comic note provided by the horned demons. The comic personality of the demons is infectious. Any few lines, if quoted in almost any company, will probably provide a certain amount of amusement:

> "In the name of heaven, Master," I cried, "what sort
> of guides are these? Let us go on alone
> if you know the way. Who can trust such an escort!

If you are as wary as you used to be
you surely see them grind their teeth at us,
and knot their beetle brows so threateningly."

XXI

Here in the first *bolgia*, the poets observe the seducers.
They make two files and are driven at an endless fast walk
by horned demons who hurry them along with great lashes.
The poets see Jason and, though Dante places him here in
Hell for punishment, he marks his majestic aspect.

"Look there, at that great soul that approaches
and seems to shed no tears for all his pain—
what kingliness moves with him even in Hell!"

XVIII

What we hear in these verses is, in fact, the voice of Dante
expressing his admiration for the man who was the first
human being to have the audacity to sail the sea. Jason was
the harbinger of the future world of navigation.

But in the second *bolgia*, the poets find the souls of the
flatterers sunk in excrement. They also observe the whore
Thaïs who "told her lover / when he sent to ask her, 'Do you
thank me much? / 'Much? Nay, past all believing!' " She is
the symbol of flattery.   XVIII

The man we follow on this journey is a man like ourselves.
Like him, we feel the sorrow of sinful love. Like him, we are
shaken by the gusts of Hell. Like him, we are disgusted by
the presence of ugly creatures. What is the secret of this
man? In the act of poetic creation Dante really believes in the
reality of what he creates: sinners, demons, monsters or ugly
creatures cease to be imaginary entities and become living
beings.

CHAPTER VII

SIMONIACS. FORTUNE TELLERS. HYPOCRITES.

Dante and Virgil come upon the third *bolgia*, and a new portentous punishment presents itself. The *bolgia* is lined with round tube-like holes, and the simoniacs are placed in them upside down with the soles of their feet ablaze. When a newcomer arrives, he crashes headlong into the hole, pushing his predecessor further down.

Here Dante creates a very dramatic situation. The name of Pope Boniface VIII rises from the hole in the rocky floor, bewildering Dante. At Virgil's bidding, Dante flings off like an insult the suggestion that he himself is Pope Boniface VIII.

Nicholas III, a predecessor of Boniface, waits for him in Hell:

> "Are you there already, Boniface? Are you there
> already?" he cried. "By several years the writ
> has lied. And all that gold, and all that care—
>
> are you already sated with the treasure
> for which you dared to turn on the Sweet Lady
> and trick and pluck and bleed her at your pleasure?"
>
> I stood like one caught in some raillery,
> not understanding what is said to him,
> lost for an answer to such mockery.
>
> XIX

This is good poetry and it is dramatic. But besides being poetic and dramatic, it is something more—it is poetry based on moral indignation.

Dante vents his moral indignation concerning the simoniac popes of his lifetime: Nicholas III, in Dante's boyhood; Boniface VIII, during Dante's active public life. It is a protest against those "ravening wolves" in the guise of shepherds, against those people who "make god of gold and silver," against those prelates who sell ecclesiastic offices to satisfy their greed.

What did Dante want? He desired a papacy freed from earthly shackles in order that it might lead and care for Christians. Temporal interests had led the popes to take a hand in worldly business and thereby to compromise their integrity. Dante wanted the Church to be solely a spiritual power. This ideal of Dante's was not to become reality until the first half of the twentieth century. The genius of Dante was to mold the future.

The fourth *bolgia* is a sorrowful and painful sight. Here the wizards and the diviners who attempted, by forbidden arts, to look into the future have their heads turned backwards on their bodies and are compelled to walk backwards.

It is a symbolic retribution. Dante's poetry finds its most varied tones in the representation of this world of spells and witchcraft. From the portrayal of the diviner Amphiareus whom "the earth swallowed before all the Thebans, / at which they cried out: 'Whither do you flee, / Amphiareus?...'" to the depiction of women "who left their spinning and sewing for soothsaying / and casting of spells with herbs, and dolls, and rags."   XX

The poets move on, talking as they go, and arrive at the fifth *bolgia*. Here the grafters are sunk in boiling pitch and guarded by demons, who tear them to pieces with claws and grappling hooks, whenever they appear above the surface of the pitch. Here we see horror piled upon horror. Fearful demons plague and punish the grafters for all eternity. Dante, like Bosch, succeeds in giving concrete and tangible shape to the popular medieval Christian conception of Hell. It is an achievement possible only for a poet of Dante's visual and dramatic power. Perhaps he could have written at the end of the canto what Jan van Eyck wrote on his peaceful scene of Arnolfini's betrothal: "I was there."

This terrifying, dramatic scene is followed by a comic scene in which the devils, bearing such names as Malacoda (Badtail), Barbariccia (Curlybeard), Cagnazzo (Deaddog), Graffiacane (Scratchdog), Ciriatto (Swineface), Ribicante (Redface), threaten Dante. Virgil hides Dante behind some rocks to protect him from the devils' wrath. Virgil secures safe-conduct from their leader, Malacoda, and he calls Dante from hiding. When the poets are about to set off, Malacoda sends a squad of demons to escort them, and Dante hears the devils talk. The devils would like to touch him on his rump, and they, whom Dante distrusts, have their own particular language, and their leader, as a sign of departure, "made a trumpet of his ass."

It is well known that Dante's vulgarity has offended certain delicate readers. But it is worth pointing out that Dante, who is a true artist, makes use of vulgarity to give the reader a true portrayal of a character. Here the devil leader wants to express his joy at the moment of departure: a joy which he expresses not through laughter, dancing or singing but through a gesture which is in unison with his depraved nature.

Dante returns to the depiction of the grafters in the pitch. He makes their presence very vivid by a beautiful simile:

> As dolphins surface and begin to flip
> their arched backs from the sea, warning the sailors
> to fall-to and begin to secure ship—
>
> So now and then, some soul, to ease his pain,
> showed us a glimpse of his back above the pitch
> and quick as lightning disappeared again.
>
> XXII

Not less vivid is the scene of two demons who start a brawl in mid-air and fall into the pitch themselves.

These lively, humorous scenes are followed by some very sad ones. It is the sixth *bolgia* where the hypocrites, weighed down by great leaden robes, walk eternally round and round a narrow track. The poets come upon Caiaphas who is punished by being himself crucified to the floor of Hell. Every sinner walks on him. Dante is intensely sensitive to the world of beauty, but he is also fascinated by the ugly, the repulsive, the very cruel. Possibly the true artist feels, as did T.S. Eliot, that "the contemplation of the horrid, or sordid or disgusting. . .is the necessary and negative aspect of the impulse toward the pursuit of beauty."[1]

The poets now discover that the bridges over the sixth *bolgia* are broken, and they cannot reach the seventh *bolgia*. Dante loses heart, but Virgil embraces him and helps him descend from boulder to boulder and Dante regains his spirits. The memory of the past danger awakens in Dante the image of the desperately poor Italian peasant who has no feed for his sheep and who, seeing the snow on the ground in the spring, thinks he is going to lose his sheep but takes heart when he realizes that the snow is only hoar-frost. This interest in delicate as well as in crude images is at the heart of everything that Dante wrote. Dante has something of the largeness of Homer and Shakespeare, though Dante reaches a depth of religious intensity unknown to both Homer and Shakespeare.

CHAPTER VIII

THIEVES. ULYSSES. FALSIFIERS.

In contrast to the slow pace of the hypocrites in the sixth *bolgia*, the seventh *bolgia* is full of movement. Here Dante finds five of his own countrymen of very noble lineage—first three in human shape, then two who are changing into ghastly reptiles. The tercets describing this transformation are graphic and intense. Sustained realism succeeds sustained realism in an atmosphere of horror and mystery unmitigated by human feeling.

This theme of transformation is already found in Ovid and Lucan, but it is Dante, well aware of the tradition, who gives it new life. The reader feels that Dante, like a sculptor, takes immense pleasure in molding and remolding reptiles from the souls of men.

Here is Vanni Fucci who has an affinity with Capaneus, (the defiant blasphemer on the burning sand) though Fucci is actually more brutal, more cynical and more insolent. His insolence is not even crushed when he is forced to confess his shameless crime of stealing the treasure from the sacristy of Pistoia. With a vigorous and dynamic style, he prophesies civil war for his native city of Pistoia and for Florence—a war that will result in the defeat of Dante's party and in Dante's lifelong exile:

> "First Pistoia is emptied of the Black,
> then Florence changes her party and her laws.
> From Valdimagra the God of War brings back
>
> a fiery vapor wrapped in turbid air:
> then in a storm of battle at Piceno
> the vapor breaks apart the mist, and there
>
> every White shall feel his wounds anew.
> And I have told you this that it may grieve you."

XXIV

The eighth *bolgia* seems like a nocturnal landscape of fireflies as they are seen by a peasant when he rests on a hill and looks into the valley. Those fireflies are in reality flames that hide the evil counselors. Here we find Ulysses, Diomedes, and others.

Dante interprets the myth of Ulysses in a new way. Homer sees in Ulysses not a criminal but a hero. If Homer glorifies the tricks of this clever Greek, Dante, versed in a Christian theology, sees Ulysses as an evildoer, a master liar, a criminal. Yet Dante, the poet, cannot resist the impulse to make him in his own likeness. Dante's passion to know all that is knowable finds outlet and personification in the figure of Ulysses.

Ulysses' quest for knowledge is a passion that commands him like a fate. Neither the fondness for his aged father, nor Penelope's claim to the joys of love could drive out of his mind "the lust to experience the far-flung world / and the failings and felicities of mankind."   XXVI

Ulysses feels this hunger for new experiences deeply, and he is also the master of a mind and a will capable of holding fast to this vision, determined to defend it against the reluctance and timidity of his companions by uttering some of the most sublime words ever spoken by man:

> "Greeks! You were not born to live like brutes,
> but to press on toward manhood and recognition!"
>   XXVI

How well these two lines express this noble view of life! How much greater than our own ordinary selves we feel here!

Dante admires Ulysses' craving for knowledge and, in contrast to the homesick Ulysses in Homer, this craving gives him a definite grandeur. But Dante is also a believer in Catholic theology that views craving for knowledge as the beginning of a bad conscience. This is the reason why Dante admires the Ulysses who breaks away from the honorable ties of home, who crosses the Mediterranean sea and who passes the bounds set by man, but Dante also punishes the great Greek by making his trip end in death in a storm before the mountain of Purgatory. Dante, as a poet, admires Ulysses but, as a student of theology, condemns him. Here Dante's imagination beats at the bars of his era and his creed. There is an unresolved conflict in his mind, but nevertheless, Dante has created a majestic figure who elicits our awe as well as our respect.

Here, in a flame that quivers and roars, is hidden Guido da Montefeltro, whose "deeds / were not of the lion but of the fox." He became a Franciscan to make amends but, nevertheless, became the victim of Pope Boniface VIII. Pope Boniface VIII, the "Prince of the New Pharisees," forced Guido to give him fraudulent advice, absolving his guilt beforehand. But when Guido died and St. Francis came to claim his soul, the devil seized it, reasoning that he who "does not repent cannot be absolved." And then, with a malicious expression,

the devil turns to St. Francis and says: "Perhaps / you
hadn't heard that I was logician."   XXVII

Dante is a creator of true characters. One of the first requi-
sites in creating memorable characters is the ability to
assign to a personage a line of poetry suitable to be spoken
by him. Logic is peculiar to the nature of man, and man is
proud of it. The devil, in speaking to a man, uses the man's
device.

Dante's visual and dramatic power is very apparent when
he describes his and Virgil's visit to the sowers of discord.
Just as their sin was to render asunder what God had meant
to be united, so are they hacked and torn throughout eternity
by a great demon with a bloody sword. The crudest figures of
this ninth *bolgia* are Mohammed, the founder of a new religion, and Bertrand de Born, the minstrel of discord. Mohammed appears cleft from chin to crotch, with his internal
organs dangling between his legs. Bertrand de Born's body
holds its severed head by its torn hair, "swinging it like a
lantern in its hand; / and the head looked at us and wept in
its despair."   XXVIII

A sensitive reader may be inclined to find the scene disgusting. But if we grant that a work of religious art, like
Dante's *Divine Comedy*, may be legitimately used to arouse
the feelings of condemnation and horror at mischief and
discord, we will admit that Dante has achieved this aim in a
masterly fashion. He has cast aside all restraint and carried
us to a pitch of emotional revulsion that no other artist has
ever accomplished.

The tenth and last *bolgia* of the eighth circle holds the
falsifiers. They are punished by afflictions of every kind, by
darkness, stench, thirst, filth and loathsome diseases.

> And as they scrubbed and clawed themselves, their nails
> drew down the scabs the way a knife scrapes bream
> or some other fish with even larger scales.
>
>   XXIX

Among the falsifiers of persons are Gianni Schicchi and

Myrrha who seized the appearance of others. Schicchi impersonated a dead man. Myrrha, moved by an incestuous passion for her father, disguised herself and slipped into his bed. They run ravening through the pit through all eternity, snatching at other souls and rending them.

The poets come across Master Adam who was a falsifier of currency, a counterfeiter. He was made "like a mandolin" because of his dropsy, with his open lips, vainly thirsting for a drop of water, while in his imagination he sees before him

> "The rivulets that run from the green flanks
> of Casentino to the Arno's flood,
> spreading their cool sweet moisture through their banks."
>
> XXX

The entire description presents us with the quintessence of what is pleasurable to our perception of scene and movement. We revel in the freshness of green hills, in the life of cool running water! Dante always makes that appeal. His subject may be ethical, political, religious—no matter how disagreeable, how abstract the idea—the appeal to our visual sense and the life-communicating movement is always there.

Dante concentrates his attention on two poor wretches, and he asks Master Adam for their names. They are Potyphar's wife who bore false witness against Joseph, and Sinon the Greek, who persuaded the Trojans to admit the Wooden Horse within their city walls. Sinon, angered by Master Adam's identification of him, strikes and abuses Master Adam with grim scorn and zeal. Master Adam replies in kind, and Dante watches, fascinated by their squabble. Virgil rebukes Dante's absorption in this noisy altercation, and Dante burns with shame. Virgil forgives him because his repentance is genuine.

CHAPTER IX

UGOLINO. SATAN.

A landscape with great towers, obscured by fog, looms before Virgil and Dante. As they draw near, they discover that the great towers are really terrible giants, who stand inside a well-pit with the upper halves of their bodies rising above the rim.

> . . .(S)o the grim giants
> whom Jove threatens when the thunder roars
>
> raised from the rim of stone about that well
> the upper halves of their bodies, which loomed up
> like turrets through the murky air of Hell.
>
> XXXI

Dante succeeds here in conveying his sense of awe to the reader. He experiences it, and, like all great artists, he also possesses the means of rendering it. Dante saw clearly that there is no better instrument for conveying awe than the combination of grimness and height.

Among these giants, Virgil identifies Nimrod, the builder of the Tower of Babel, who speaks a language no one understands. There is also Antaeus, who takes the poets in his huge palm and lowers them to the first round of the ninth circle, Cocytus, and "then straightened like a mast above a ship." The verse is keenly mimetic and it depicts the movement as well as the height of the giant.   XXXI

Antaeus has deposited the poets in the huge frozen lake, Cocytus, which is divided into four rounds, each named for a famous traitor in history. Caina holds those treacherous to their kin; the Antenora, those treacherous to their country; the Ptolomea, those treacherous to their guests; the Judecca, those treacherous to their masters.

The landscape of Cocytus is a landscape of frozen ugliness. The sinners are buried in ice, and the ice blocks every movement they try to make, and when they start crying, their tears congeal and they are forced to shut their eyes, which become completely frozen. The sinners attempt to open their eyes but to no avail. But this terribly ugly world is animated by Dante's political passion, which takes form in cruel imagery. Dante accidentally kicks the head of Bocca degli Abati, the man who had betrayed Dante's faction at the battle of Montaperti. Dante proceeds to grab him by the hair, twisting it in his hand, tearing out more than one tuft of it. Vast and varied feelings gather in Dante's soul in this frozen setting which punishes the greatest of sins, in Dante's view, treason.

Cocytus is the setting of the most pathetic and dramatic episode of the *Inferno*, the episode of Ugolino. Ugolino was accused of treason by the Pisans, and he and his children were shut in a tower and left to die from hunger.

The episode is the tragedy of innocence. The children are helpless. It is the tragedy of paternal love, for Ugolino suffers more from his children's fate than from his own. It is the tragedy of absolute despair expressed in Ugolino's unforgettable words:

> "I did not weep: I had turned stone inside.
> They wept. 'What ails you, Father, you look so strange,'
> my little Anselm, youngest of them cried."

XXXIII

Then comes the death of all four children, one after another.

> "Gaddo, the eldest, fell before me and cried,
> stretched at my feet upon that prison floor:
> 'Father, why don't you help me?' There he died."

XXXIII

Dante's tragic imagination has deepened. Ugolino is a traitor, and, therefore, is punished with death, but when he is forced to watch the slow agony of his innocent children, we can no longer think of him as a traitor. We begin to marvel at what this man must tolerate, at what this man must endure. Ugolino is now like some peak of anguish, an anguish that comes close to redemption.

And finally Dante and Virgil see Satan in the distance. The monster looks "like a whirling windmill seen afar at twilight, / or when a mist has risen from the ground."

XXXIV

The represenstation of Satan engulfs the reader in accumulating terror. Satan has three faces, one face is fiery red, the other is between white and yellow, the third is black. Satan has six eyes, three mouths, six wings, and it is the beating of these wings that is the source of the icy wind of Cocytus. Satan "In every mouth he worked a broken sinner / between his rake-like teeth. Thus he kept three / in eternal pain at his eternal dinner." The sinners are Judas, the betrayer of Christ, and Brutus and Cassius, the betrayers of Caesar, that is, of the Roman Empire.

XXXIV

The infernal trip has come to an end. Virgil, with Dante on his shoulders, grapples on the hair of Satan and, with great effort, reaches the center of the earth, "the point to which all gravities are drawn," and, then, turning around, begins to climb toward the opposite hemisphere until he emerges from Hell. Before emerging Virgil and Dante notice that Satan is upside down in the infernal tomb. There he fell from Heaven when the Lord, after the rebellion of the angels, hurled him headlong into the abyss. "[A]nd the land that spread here once hid in the sea / and fled North to our hemisphere for fright."   XXXIV

In the darkness, the poets hear the sound of a rivulet, which indicates the hidden path they must take in order to see the world of light. They push on without rest, till they emerge once more to see the stars.

PURGATORIO

CHAPTER X

CATO. MANFRED.

The sweet light has reappeared, the nightmare of the starless air is over. Dante revels in the sight of the rediscovered sun.

> Sweet azure of the sapphire of the east
> was gathering on the serene horizon
> its pure and perfect radiance—a feast
>
> to my glad eyes, reborn to their delight. . .

I

This stress on light permeates the whole atmosphere of the

first canto of the Purgatorio* and colors everything with a
memorable freshness from the depiction of the sun and the
stars to the description of the dawn. "The dawn, in triumph,
made the day-breeze flee / before its coming, so that from
afar / I recognized the trembling of the sea."   I

Dante, like all the great exponents of civilization, from
Vermeer to Goethe, has been driven on, step by step, by his
impulse to see everything clearly—hence, his stress on light.
In Dante this visual power reaches its highest point in this
canto. He does not give us the essence of things but their
presence; he does not give us the nature of things but their
live sensations.

The poets reach the rugged mountain of Purgatory and are
dismayed to find that it is a sheer rise and "the nimblest legs
/ would not have served, unless they walked on air."   III
Dante eagerly looks at the stars, and then he sees an ancient
man of impressive bearing. The ancient man is Cato of
Utica, the guardian of Purgatory. Cato challenges the poets
as fugitives from Hell, but Virgil, after instructing Dante to
kneel in reverence, explains Dante's mission:

> "Now may his coming please you, for he goes
> to win his freedom; and how dear that is
> the man who gives his life for it best knows."
>
>   I

What we normally hear in the dramatic dialogue is the

*When I was a college student, I was very enthusiastic about the
Inferno. The *Inferno is certainly a very poetical world with its
powerful sinners, profound passions, incredible settings. But as I
grew older, I became less enthusiastic about it, and I found myself
more at ease with the Purgatorio.* My preference certainly did not
mean that I thought the *Purgatorio* better poetry. The source of
enjoyment of the *Purgatorio* was the intimate world of Dante. The
Purgatorio is crowded with Dante's friends, from Casella to Belacqua, from Nino de Visconti to Forese. It seems that Dante, as he
continued to work on the *Comedy* and as the years went by, felt the
need to surround himself with familiar and dear faces to overcome
the loneliness and bitterness of his exile.

voice of Dante himself, who has put on the costume and demeanor of Virgil. Dante, like Cato who committed suicide to escape the tyranny of Caesar, looks for freedom from the slavery of sin. He looks to the sons of light for freedom from the world of incontinence, violence and fraud to the realm of intelligence enlightened by faith.

Dante sees a light approaching at enormous speed across the sea. The light grows and becomes visible. It is the angel boatman who ferries the souls of the elect from the mouth of the Tiber to the shore of the mountain of Purgatory: ". . .he scorns man's tools: he needs no oars / nor any other sail than his own wings / to carry him between such distant shores."

II

The souls disembark and then, swiftly as the angel has come, he is gone. The angel, who makes use of his wings to move the boat, is silent. It is with this silence that Dante conveys the angel's majesty. His truth needs no words.

Dante, after seeing the horror of Hell and after shedding many a tear before visions of the sorrow and pain of sinful souls, now needs some relief and comfort. This need takes the form of the encounter between Dante and his friend, the musician Casella. It is Casella who, at the request of Dante, strikes up one of Dante's own songs: "Amore che nella mente mi ragiona," "Love that speaks its reasons in my heart." II

It is a beautiful song, which seems to realize itself first as a particular rhythm before it reaches expression in words. The rhythm brings joy to the souls who, by listening, put off their future purification. Cato descends upon the souls, berating them, and like startled pigeons, they scatter and start climbing the slope toward the mountain:

> Exactly as a flock of pigeons gleaning
> a field of stubble, pecking busily,
> forgetting all their primping and their preening,
>
> will rise as one and scatter through the air,
> leaving their feast without another thought
> when they are taken by a sudden scare

so that new band, all thought of pleasure gone,
broke from the feast of music with a start
and scattered for the mountainside like one

who leaps and does not look where he will land.

II

These souls are obedient but also timid because they have just arrived in Purgatory and are overpowered by this new mysterious world. And Dante, whose wisdom seems to spring from a spiritual source, and who has acquired a depth of observation from having lived with human beings in all walks of life, compares these souls to sheep: "As sheep come through a gate—by ones, by twos, / by threes, and all the others trail behind, / timidly, nose to the ground . . ."   III

Now Dante introduces a very moving scene that reveals his sympathy for Manfred, the king of Sicily, who died a tragic death at the battle of Benevento. The king, who had been excommunicated by the Church, is here waiting at the base of the cliff to begin his purification, to expiate his "horrible" sins. Manfred narrates how, at the point of death, he begged for God's forgiveness, the God whose "abiding Goodness . . . holds out / its open arms to all who turn" to Him. Thus he is saved.   III

The narration is beautiful, but what transcends place and time and is capable of arousing a direct response of man to man, in readers of any place and time, is Manfred's evocation of a world full of lugubrious beauty. His bones, once buried under the heavy guard of a stone mound, were transported from the battlefield by the bishop of Cosenza with tapers quenched and now these bones are "rattled by the wind, by the rain drenched."

But as our reading of the episode continues, and our powers of reflection become stronger, we are struck by the character of Manfred. The fierce warrior's tenderness is now for his living daughter Constance, and he begs Dante to bear a message to her in order that she may offer prayer for his soul and, thereby, shorten his period of waiting. Though we may at this stage appreciate Manfred's character, we are also impressed by his moral attitude, for he has forgiven his enemies. In a world in which many individuals are incapable of forgiveness, Manfred sets a Christian example. In a world in which the prevalent style runs more to the cold eye of the avenger, to a numb remorselessness, Manfred shows that forgiveness is an impulse that releases man from the chains of the past and makes him free.

Dante's style adds further beauty to the episode. The verses are built with the simplest words in the most colloquial idiom. Only a poet of great artistic experience is capable of such lines:

> And one soul said to me: "Whoever you are,
> as you move on, look back and ask yourself
> if you have ever seen me over there."
> . . .
>
> When I, in all humility, confessed
> I never before had seen him, he said, "Look"
> —and showed me a great slash above his breast.

III

There is nothing so simple and sure in Dante's work. It is true that later this colloquial style glides into a formal one but, nevertheless, we retain the impression that the language of conversation has been raised to great poetry.

CHAPTER XI

BELACQUA. BUONCONTE. SORDELLO.

Indolence, the extreme indisposition to labor, finds its personification in the interesting figure of Belacqua. What makes a figure interesting? It is either the representation of the emotional forces of the human soul or the presence of humor. Humor, indeed, is the characteristic of the Belacqua episode. This friend of Dante's, who was the laziest man in Florence, found the time to repent before he died. The man, who put off good works and the active desire for grace in life, has now returned to his old, lazy habit in the Hereafter. "Maybe by that time / you'll find you need to sit before you fly!" Belacqua even tries to explain the reason for his philosophy of life.

"Old friend," he said, "what good is it to climb?—
God's Bird above the Gate would never let me
pass through to start my trials before my time."

IV

A new lyrical theme, the product of political partisanship,
deals with the death of Buonconte of Montefeltro and the
serious misfortune that befell his body. Having disappeared
in the battle of Campaldino, his "throat pierced through,
fleeing on foot / and staining all (his) course with (his) life's
blood," Buonconte reached the stream Archiana, and there
he died, moaning the name of Mary and thus was saved. But
the demon, who could not have his body, began to torture it
by stirring up an enormous storm.   V

The description of the storm is very poetical. Dante has the
ability to give a perfect and unique pattern to every tercet,
such that the full beauty of the description of the storm is
found in every detail; the saturated air changes into rain, the
rain floods the ditches, the rivulets, the river Archiana,
which, raging froth and mud, sweeps the body into the Arno.

Here we find the theme of the noblewoman Pia dei Tolo-
mei. She begs Dante to remember her on his return to earth
after he has rested from the long journey:

A third spoke when that second soul had done:
"When you have found your way back to the world, and
found your rest from this long road you run,

oh speak my name again with living breath to living
memory. Pia am I."

V

Dante creates a delicate character by stressing Pia's sis-
terly concern for him as well as by giving a soft tone to the
words spoken by Pia. " 'Deh, quando tu sarai tornato al
mondo / e riposato della lunga via ... / ricordati di me, che
son la Pia....' " Pia's words are so soft that they seem rather
sighed than spoken. We can never emulate music because to

arrive at the condition of music would be the annihilation of poetry. But it is also true that only by emulating some aspects of music—the soft or harsh tone—can we express the cruelty, the ferocity, the reticence, the delicacy of a character.

Virgil and Dante press on, and there on the shady slope they encounter the soul of the poet Sordello who, like Virgil, is a Mantuan. Sordello asks in what country the poets were born and who they were.

> My gentle Guide began:
> "Mantua. . ." And that shade, till then withdrawn,
>
> leaped to his feet like one in sudden haste
> crying: "O Mantuan, I am Sordello
> of your own country!" And the two embraced.
>
> VI

This scene, which stresses the love for one's land, has an autobiographical quality. Dante, who was an exile for almost twenty years in different Italian cities, far from his beloved Florence, must have occasionally met some of his countrymen in these places. The scene is too realistic and deeply felt not to be connected with Dante's life experiences.

This act of Sordello's prods Dante to write a pathetic, rapid invective against war-torn Italy whose children, who should have the same feeling for each other as that felt by Sordello for Virgil, fight against each other:

> Ah servile Italy, grief's hostelry,
> ah ship unpiloted in the storm's rage,
> no mother of provinces but of harlotry!
>
> VI

This invective against the political chaos of Italy demonstrates the deep hatred already strong in the thought of Dante. That hatred developed still further with Machiavelli and Alfieri until it became the characteristic feature of the Italian Risorgimento. It affected every aspect of Italian life,

be it literary, historical or philosophical. Italian regional-
isms were abandoned, and there arose an intense desire for
Italian unification, which finally took place in the nine-
teenth century.

An idyllic state of mind now overtakes Dante, and he beau-
tifully describes the Flowering Valley in which he places the
negligent rulers:

> Nor has glad Nature only colored there,
> but of a thousand sweet scents made a single
> earthless, nameless fragrance of the air.
>
> VII

Dante seems to have been in love with nature all his life, with
the wide pastures and green fields, with the wild life or birds,
beasts, flowers, with the cheerful sunrise and the sad sunset.

It is here that Dante gives us the most poetic sunset in all
literature. For the poets it was the time of the day when the
souls of sailor and traveler look back in longing for their
homes:

> It was the hour that turns the memories
> of sailing men their first day out, to home,
> and friends they sailed from on that morning's breeze;
>
> that thrills the traveler newly on his way
> with love and yearning when he hears afar
> the bell that seems to mourn the dying day
>
> VIII

The verses are very lyrical. Dante associates the circumstances of time and place, a doctrine or a truth with the sweet
sensations these things evoke in our minds.

CHAPTER XII

THE ANGEL GUARDIAN.
THE ENVIOUS.

Dawn is approaching. "At that new hour when the first dawn light grows / and the little swallow starts her mournful cry."
                                                                    IX

It is during this dawn that Dante has a dream of a golden eagle that descends from the height of Heaven and carries him to the sphere of Fire. He wakes to find that he has been transported in his sleep, that it was the saint Lucia who bore him and deposited him before the gate of Purgatory. Seated there on the topmost of three steps is the angel guardian who holds a drawn sword. The three steps symbolize the three parts of a perfect act of confession and the sword, the idea of justice.

Some critics, including John D. Sinclair, have criticized Dante's portrayal of the angel guardian as too symbolical in

a "tedious and irksome"[1] way to be a poetical figure, saying
also that the angel guardian lacks reality. But the fact is that
the angel guardian does not have to be real. If he is a mere
symbol, the symbol of the sacrament of penance, he does not
have to have the traits of an ordinary human being, deter-
minate feelings, specific thoughts or individual physical
characteristics. If the angel guardian were more particular-
ized, he would be false.

Dante prostrates himself at the feet of the angel guardian,
who cuts seven P's (for "peccata" or sins in Latin) in Dante's
forehead with the point of a blazing sword. The cuts indicate
the seven deadly sins from which Dante must be purged, and
seven are the cornices (ledges) of the mountain of Purgatory,
which correspond to the seven deadly sins. In the Purgatory,
which is the realm of expiation, the seven deadly sins are
contrasted with the seven virtues: pride with humility; envy
with charity; wrath with meekness; sloth with zeal; avarice
and prodigality with liberality; gluttony with temperance;
lust with chastity. Here Dante expresses in poetic form the
ethical system uttered by the theologians in their writings,
by the mystics in their prayers, and by the craftsmen in their
churches.

Dante loves images that are suggestive of movement, and
while ascending a rocky path, the poets come upon three
marvelous scenes of humility carved in the face of the cliff.

The first scene depicts the angel's Annunciation to Mary.
The angel

> stood carved before us with such force and love,
> with such a living grace in his whole pose,
> the image seemed about to speak and move.
>
> . . .
> Mary's flowing gesture seemed to say—
> impressed there as distinctly as a seal
> impresses wax—*Ecce ancilla Dei.*

X

Another scene shows the humble king David dancing with
hiked up robes before the Ark. The last scene represents the

emperor Trajan en route to war—a widow, "in tears wept from the long grief of the poor," implores the emperor to secure justice on behalf of her murdered son, while the eagles of the great golden banners "seemed to flutter in the wind." The emperor dismounts his horse and administers justice to the poor woman.

Then Virgil calls attention to a band of souls approaching from the left, and Dante turns for his first sight of the souls of the proud, who crawl agonizingly round and round the cornice, under the crushing weight of enormous slabs of rock.

The cornice of the proud contains two important themes, the first is the paraphrasing of the Lord's Prayer. Its traditional words assume a fresh meaning as elaborated in Dante.

> "Let come to us the sweet peace of Thy reign,
> for if it come not we cannot ourselves
> attain to it however much we strain
>
> . . .
> . . .As we forgive our trespassers the ill
> we have endured, do Thou forgive, not weighing
> our merits, but the mercy of Thy will."

XI

Why does Dante write beautiful religious verses? Why does he reach the highest level of poetry? People writing poetry are usually writing as they want to feel. Their poetry is the result of reflection, effort, hard work. But Dante writes poetry the way he really feels, spontaneously, and, therefore, his poetry is truly beautiful.

The second theme, the theme of the vanity of human glory, Dante puts on the lips of Oderisi d'Agobbio, who was once a famous illustrator of manuscripts, but whose fame is now exceeded by that of Franco Bolognese.

> "A breath of wind is all there is to fame
> here upon earth: it blows this way and that,
> and when it changes quarter it changes name."

XI

Oderisi is a true character because Dante assigns to this personage lines of poetry very suitable to him.

The poets reach the second cornice where they come upon the souls of the envious. Dante describes their punishment. They offended with their eyes, envying all the good they saw of others, and, therefore, their eyes are wired shut. Mysterious voices cry out examples of glorified charity and punished envy.

Among these mysterious voices the poets hear Cain's tragic "voice" that suddenly "ripped like lightning" and struck at them with a cry, "All men are my destroyers!" With Dante here, far more than with any other poet, the word combination offers perpetual novelty. It enlarges the meaning of the individual words. The word "voce" combined with the word "folgore," for example, increases in significance.

XIV

CHAPTER XIII

VISIONS. MARCO LOMBARDO.
THE SIREN.

The poets are walking straight into the sun, when a great radiance blinds Dante and he finds himself in the presence of the angel of charity. Dante compares the angel's radiance, which blinds him, to the reflection of a sunbeam striking a mirror or a pool of water, a fresh comparison that clearly depicts the sensuous effect of the light on the eye.

Virgil and Dante are entranced by three visions that extol the opposite of wrath, the virtue of meekness. In the first vision, Mary looks for her son. " 'My son, my son, why do you treat us so? / Your father and I were seeking you in tears.' " In the second vision, a young man loves and wishes to marry Pisistratus's daughter. Though he has not won the parents' consent, he embraces the young girl in public. The wife of Pisistratus, full of anger, demands that her husband avenge himself "on the presumptuous one / who dared embrace our daughter." And Pisistratus answers " 'What shall we do to those that wish us harm, if we take vengeance upon those that love us?' " In the third vision, the first Christian martyr Stephen is being stoned by a hate-filled crowd which is roaring " 'Kill! Kill!' " but the martyr, "his death / already heavy on him" prays God to forgive his murderers.   XV

These visions are not real; Dante realizes that they are the product of his imagination. Nevertheless, they shed some light on his character. Dante had a temperament much subject to wrath, and he needed the inward persuasion of great examples of meekness so that he may open his heart and gain interior peace.

Virgil and Dante move on, and they observe an enormous cloud of smoke ahead of them. They are in the third cornice where the air is like the darkness of Hell or a night devoid of planets. Here are the wrathful. The smoke stings the eyes as wrath corrodes the soul. As wrath obscures human reason, so the souls are plunged into darkness.

A new theme of political passion arises in the figure of Marco Lombardo. Dante makes this unknown man the spokesman for the necessity of having an emperor, so that the sun of the emperor may shine beside the sun of the Church. Here we find the assertion of Dante's political and religious theory.

> "Rome used to shine in two suns which her rod
> made the world good, and each showed her its way:
> one to the ordered world, and one to God."
>
>   XVI

Dante, in the guise of Marco, maintains that Church and Empire are not sun and moon but "two suns," each holding commission and authority from God Himself.

Dante's great poem sums up the essential ideas of the Catholic Church and represents a literary counterpart to the philosophic synthesis of St. Thomas. But if we turn to the figure of Marco Lombardo, we see that Dante's political and religious views differ widely from those of St. Thomas and even more from those of St. Augustine. Here for the first time in Christian thought, we find the earthly and temporal city regarded as an autonomous order with its own supreme end, which is not the service of the Church but the realization of all the natural potentialities of human culture.

Dante is nevertheless influenced most powerfully by St. Thomas's ideas with regard to the problem of free will. For Marco, and therefore for Dante, if the world goes wrong, the cause is to be found in man and not in the stars.

> "The spheres *do* start your impulses along.
> I do not say *all*, but suppose I did—
> the light of reason still tells right from wrong."
>
>   XVI

For Dante and St. Thomas our actions are not determined by the stars but by our capacity to choose between good and evil.

Certainly Dante was of his age. There is no man who is more medieval than Dante, in his immense faith, his intolerance, his symbolism, and in his hierarchical view of society. We can hardly ignore the fact that Dante was born and lived in that particular time and place. But we must also remember that a man who represents his age can also be battling with it. Against the popular view that man's actions are determined by the stars, Dante asserts human responsibility. Against the practice of princes and administrators who kept astrologers in their service, Dante defends the pivotal role of reason.

In the fourth cornice Dante and Virgil meet the slothful, the souls of those who recognized the Good but were not diligent in pursuit of it. Two souls run before the rest, one shouting aloud and citing Mary as an example of holy zeal, the other citing Caesar as an example of temporal zeal.

There are moments of pure poetry in this cornice. Dante,

his head full of confused thoughts, sinks into sleep. Instantly,
his thoughts are transformed into a dream.

> Then when those shades had drawn so far ahead
> that I could not make out a trace of them,
> a new thought seized upon me, and it bred
>
> so many more, so various, and so scrambled,
> that turning round and round inside itself
> so many ways at once, my reason rambled;
>
> I closed my eyes and all that tangled theme
> was instantly transformed into a dream.

XVIII

Dante dreams of the Siren who is a "stuttering crone, /
squint-eyed, clubfooted, both her hands deformed, / and her
complexion like a whitewashed stone." The Siren, who lured
Ulysses from his course, symbolizes avarice, gluttony and
lust, the sins that are expiated in the following cornices. A
Heavenly Lady helps Dante in his dream, and when he
wakens, "[a]lready the high day / lit all the circles of the holy
mountain." Dante and Virgil resume the journey. The angel
of zeal "[w]ith swanlike wings outspread" shows them the
passage to the fifth cornice. Here, as in many other verses,
Dante has a strongly individual idiom. He coins new words,
discovers new sounds and conceives new similes.   XIX

CHAPTER XIV

HOARDERS AND WASTERS. STATIUS. THE GLUTTONS.

Dante and Virgil continue their journey, and they reach the fifth cornice where they see the souls of the hoarders and wasters, who lie motionless and outstretched, bound hand and foot. As in life, they turned their souls away from God with an inordinate concern for material things; now they lie with their faces in the dust.

Among these hoarders Dante notices the Pope Adrian V. The Pope tells Dante how he was elected and how he gave up his avarice when he saw the falseness of the world.

84

"My conversion, alas, came late; for only when
I had been chosen Pastor of Holy Rome
did I see the falseness in the lives of men.

I saw no heart's rest there, nor ease from strife,
nor any height the flesh-bound soul might climb,
and so I came to love this other life."

XIX

The character of Adrian is real for us because he is treated with the understanding of love. Dante and Adrian share the same ethical views. There are some critics who put "ethical poetry" on the defensive. For too many people the expression of ethical views has become something to apologize for on the ground that poetry should express feelings—love, hatred, anger. But to understand Dante, we must recognize that his view of ethics was not merely an idea, it was a deeply felt reality.

The theme of political passion returns. One of the sinners identifies himself as Hugh Capet, and proceeds to a denunciation of the Capetian kings, the dynasty he himself founded, but which has degenerated into a succession of rulers distinguished only for their bloodthirsty avarice.

Here Dante, whose heart is full of hostility toward the Capetian kings for confronting and undermining the Empire, for debasing and subjugating the Church, for plotting and scheming in the affairs of Italy, puts on the lips of Hugh Capet the following verses:

"O God, my Lord, when shall my soul rejoice
to see Thy retribution, which, lying hidden,
sweetens Thine anger in Thy secret choice?"

XX

Dante puts politics into verses, and though in "political, poetry" thought has primacy over inspiration, he still succeeds as a poet. Dante has that strange gift, so rarely bestowed, for turning thought into feeling.

Dante has hardly left Hugh Capet when he feels the moun-

tain shake as if stricken by an earthquake. A chill seizes
Dante as seizes one that goes to death, but Virgil reassures
him. The poets move at top speed, but Dante remains deep in
thought, his mind pondering this new phenomenon.

The earthquake occurs when a soul arises from its final
purification and begins its ascent to heaven. Thus nature
participates in the ascent to heaven. The purified soul is
Statius, the Roman poet, who, from now on, will accompany
Dante and Virgil through Purgatory.

The encounter between Virgil and Statius is one of the
most original scenes of the *Divine Comedy*. It is warm with
affection, reverence, and playfulness. To have lived in Virgil's time, says Statius, he would have endured another year
of the pains he has just ended. Virgil's glance checks the
smile that rises on Dante's face at these words, but not before
Statius has caught the flash upon his features and asks
Dante to explain. Dante informs him that he is, indeed, in
the presence of Virgil. Statius forgets that he and Virgil are
empty shades, and drops to kiss his master's feet.

Dante must have fantasized about his beloved Virgil
many times during his lonely exile. I have no doubt that
Dante, when he wrote the lines below, assumed the role of
Statius to relive his own strong love for Virgil. Dante saw
him as his "favorite author" and, in the fourth *Eclogue,* as the
harbinger of Christianity. Let us listen to Statius' address to
Virgil:

> "You were the lamp that led me from that night.
> You led me forth to drink Parnassian waters;
> then on the road to God you shed your light.
>
> When you declared, 'A new birth has been given.
> Justice returns, and the first age of man.
> And a new progeny descends from Heaven'—
>
> You were as one who leads through a dark track
> holding the light behind—useless to you,
> precious to those who followed at your back."

XXII

The fact that the generally great love for Virgil in the
Middle Ages was a mixture of love and magic must not be
allowed to obscure the originality with which Dante conceived the scene. There is, I think, no precedent for the spirit
of the scene; and the attitude toward the classics, which is
there expressed, is something that we ought to find particularly intelligible now, when there is a movement to return to
a more traditional curriculum in colleges and universities. It
was Dante who taught us the beauty of the classical world
with its literature and laws; it is from Dante that we inherit
the perception of the grandeur of the classical world with its
arts and administrative skills.

The three poets leave the fifth cornice and arrive at the
sixth one. This is the cornice of the gluttons; and the poets
encounter an enormous tree laden with fruits and a clear
cascade.

> But soon, in mid-road, there appeared a tree
> laden with fragrant and delicious fruit,
> . . .
> From that side where the cliff closed-off our way
> a clear cascade fell from the towering rock
> and broke upon the upper leaves as spray.
>
> XXII

The gluttons, who hear mysterious voices crying out the
great examples of abstinence, cannot either touch the fruits,
or drink the water.

Here Dante is in contact with the life of things, the fragrance of fruits, the clarity and freshness of water. There is
only one parallel to Dante's world, and though it is a daring
one, it is a comparison not unfair to Dante. It is the several
passages of Virgil's *Georgics* in which the Roman poet describes the beauty of the dark shadows of the forest, the
coolness of the evening breeze, and the song of the goldfinch
in the bushes.

Among the gluttons who are pale and emaciated, Dante
recognizes his old friend, the poet Forese who, before deliver-

ing a salty invective against the immodest women of Florence, pays homage to his widow Nella because she prays for him and who has advanced him in Purgatory and directly to this cornice:

> "My Nella's flood of tears," he answered me,
> "have borne me up so soon to let me drink
> the blessed wormwood of my agony.
>
> Her sighs and prayers were heard where Love abounds:
> they raised me from the slope where I lay waiting
> and set me free of all the other Rounds.
>
> The dearer and more pleasing in God's sight
> is the poor widow of my love, as she
> is most alone in doing what is right."
>
> XXIII

What makes these verses more poetical than some other Dantean verses is, I think, that the subject matter gives Dante an adequate object for genuine emotion. The emotion is the love of family life; and since this emotion was reinforced by Dante's own lack of family life, it acquires a definite intensity. It is difficult, in considering Dante's poetry, not to go into the analysis of the man. A man who lives without the members of his family is bound to become a glorifier of domestic life.

CHAPTER XV

BONAGIUNTA. GUINIZELLI.
LEAH AND RACHEL.

Virgil, Statius, and Dante move on as Dante continues his talk with Forese, who identifies many of the souls who expiate the sin of gluttony. One of these souls is the poet Bonagiunta da Lucca.

Bonagiunta turns to Dante with his flattering question:

> "But is this really the creator of
> those new *canzoni*, one of which begins
> 'Ladies who have the intellect of Love'?"

XXIV

Dante answers without mentioning his name:

> And I: "When Love inspires me with delight,
> or pain, or longing, I take careful note,
> and as he dictates in my soul, I write."

XXIV

Bonagiunta, having by now become fully aware of Dante's name and the nature of the poetry Dante has cultivated, and recognizing the difference between the poetry of his School and that of Dante, answers this way:

> "Ah, brother, now I see the thong
> that held Guittone, and the Judge, and me
> short of that sweet new style of purest song.
>
> I see well how your pens attained such powers
> by following exactly Love's dictation,
> which certainly could not be said of ours."

XXIV

Bonagiunta clearly states the difference between the artificial poetry of his School and the School of the Sweet New Style of which Dante is a representative. In a truly poetic work, the poet is only concerned with expressing in verse the obscure impulse of his feeling so that the process may exorcise the demon in his soul.

The three poets move ahead and meet the angel of abstinence who, with his wing, removes one of the "P's" cut into Dante's forehead when he entered Purgatory.

> Soft on my brow I felt a zephyr pass,
> soft as those airs of May that herald dawn
> with breathing fragrances of flowers and grass;
>
> and unmistakably I felt the brush
> of the soft wing releasing to my senses
> ambrosial fragrances in a soft rush.

XXIV

Dante gives us a simile in which tactile and olfactory sensations are very nearly fused and fused together with the
thought.

The poets reach the seventh and last cornice where the
lustful, wrapped in sheets of flame, are punished. They cry
out in praise of an example of high chastity.

Here Dante meets the poet Guido Guinizelli. It is an
encounter in which Dante pays homage to him as the father
of the Sweet New Style.

> And I to him: "Your songs so sweet and clear
> which, for as long as modern usage lives,
> shall make the very ink that writes them dear."
>
> XXVI

This homage to Guinizelli expresses Dante's deep sense of
fellowship with other poets. We may recall his first meeting
with Virgil in the wood, his reception as one of their number
by the great poets of antiquity in Limbo, Sordello's amazing
greeting of Virgil in Anti-Purgatory, and the startling
encounter between Statius and Virgil.

Guinizelli withdraws, and Dante addresses Arnault Daniel
who answers in the Provençal language and begs that
Dante say a prayer for him. But now the poets have come to
the farthest limit of the seventh cornice. They are greeted by
the angel of chastity who tells them that they must pass the
wall of fire. Dante remains deaf to all Virgil's appeals, until
the utterance of Beatrice's name at last overcomes his reluctance. Night overtakes the poets, and they lie down, each on
the step on which he finds himself.

The journey through pains and torments has come to an
end, and an image of tranquillity fills Dante's soul. Dante
gazes at the stars after a difficult journey, as a shepherd
"covers" his goats "with his eye" after a tiring day.

> As goats on a rocky hill will dance and leap,
> nimble and gay, till they find grass, and then,
> while they are grazing, grow as tame as sheep

at ease in the green shade when the sun is high
and the shepherd stands by, leaning on his staff,
and at his ease covers them with his eye—.

XXVII

Dante is one of the few poets in whom the language of his
mature years is as beautiful as that of his young years. It sets
Dante in a very small class which includes Shakespeare and
very few others.

The poets are now tired, and they fall asleep. In his sleep
Dante has a dream of the sisters Leah and Rachel. Leah is
the symbol of active life; Rachel is the symbol of contemplative life. But one of these symbols ceases to be a symbol and
becomes a poetic image. Leah is an innocent and beautiful
maiden who walks a sunny field, gathering flowers, moving
her hands to weave garlands for herself and caroling as she
goes—for a painter like Botticelli one could imagine no better
subject than this caroling, garland-weaving creature:

> "Say I am Leah if any ask my name,
> and my white hands weave garlands wreath on wreath
> to please me when I stand before the frame
>
> of my bright glass. For this my fingers play
> among these blooms. But my sweet sister Rachel
> sits at her mirror motionless all day.
>
> To stare into her own eyes endlessly
> is all her joy, as mine is in my weaving.
> She looks, I do. Thus live we joyously."

XXVII

Dante, in his mature years, has created a poetic figure
which is the result of his deep feeling and interest in feminine beauty. It is difficult to generalize about human behavior, but one thing seems certain: the common man grows
intellectually with time, while his emotions weaken; but the
true poet retains the freshness and intensity of his youthful
emotions.

CHAPTER XVI

VIRGIL. MATILDA. BEATRICE.

The dawn arrives, and the poets rise and race up the rest of the ascent until they come in sight of the Earthly Paradise.

By now Virgil's task has been accomplished. He has now come to the limit of reason and he can no longer understand this world where the glory of Christianity will be represented, the Christianity that he never knew. Virgil speaks his final words to Dante:

> "Expect no more of me in word or deed:
> here your will is upright, free, and whole,
> and you would be in error not to heed
>
> whatever your own impulse prompts you to:
> lord of yourself I crown and mitre you."

XXVII

93

These verses are both beautiful and full of wisdom. Our guides, our teachers, our parents, nourish our minds with their thoughts and guidance, but the time does come when we must stand alone in order to acquire that self-reliance and independence which are the traits of a true personality.

Dante now wanders at his leisure into the Earthly Paradise where God created Adam and Eve before the original sin. He celebrates the infancy of things, the freshness of the newly created world in the words that sing "the luxuriant holy forest evergreen," the sweet air that strikes one's face, the swaying of the trembling branches, the small birds twittering on the top of the trees, the flowing river Lethe, "its wavelets bending back / the grasses on its banks as if in play."　　　　　　　　　　　　　　　　　　　　　　XXVIII

The poetry of the Earthly Paradise finds its ultimate expression in the appearance of Matilda:

> a lady, all alone, who wandered there
> singing, and picking flowers from the profusion
> with which her path was painted everywhere
> . . . .
>
> As a dancer, keeping both feet on the ground
> and close together, hardly putting one
> before the other, spins herself around—
>
> so did she turn to me upon the red
> and yellow flowerlets, virgin modesty
> making her lower her eyes and bow her head.
>
> 　　　　　　　　　　　　　　　　　　　　　XXVIII

The more one reflects on these verses, the more one must concede Dante's sensitivity to feminine charm. The Greeks, to quote Berenson, "felt this charm, and expressed it in many a terra cotta figurine which still survives to delight us,"[1] as well as in Homer's Nausicaa.* Then many centuries

---

*Nausicaa is a maiden who befriended the stranded Odysseus in the Homeric epic *Odyssey*.

intervened during which the charms of femininity remained unrecorded, and, until the thirteenth century, nothing appeared except for the great *Divine Comedy*.

Matilda, singing like a woman in love, moves upstream along one bank of the Lethe, and Dante keeps pace with her on the other side. A glorious light and a sweet melody grow in the air, filling Dante with rapture. Heavenly signs appear—seven candelabra, which seem to be seven golden trees. Then comes the procession of twenty-four elders, followed by four beasts who guard a triumphant chariot drawn by a griffon who, with the fore parts of an eagle and the hind parts of a lion, represents the divine and human nature of Christ.

There are ecclesiastic allegories here. At the right wheel of the chariot symbolizing the Church, dance three maidens who represent the three theological virtues; at its left come four maidens who symbolize the four cardinal virtues. This group is followed by two elders representing Luke as the author of *Acts* and Paul as the author of the four *Epistles*; by four elders representing James, Peter, John and Jude as authors of the four *Catholic Epistles*; and finally by a single elder representing John as the author of *Revelation*. And all these seven elders were robed like the first twenty-four "in flowing robes of white, but, for their crowns, / it was not wreaths of lillies that they wore, / but roses and whatever blooms most red."   XXIX

It seems to me that Dante finds himself at a disadvantage here. He is dealing with allegories, symbols of abstract thought, and abstract thought is, by its very nature, refractory to poetry. Nevertheless, Dante infuses some poetry by creating an arcane and mysterious atmosphere.

The procession is the prelude to the appearance of Beatrice who appears on the left side of the chariot, half-hidden from view by showers of blossoms poured from above by a hundred angels:

> Exactly so, within a cloud of flowers
> that rose like fountains from the angels' hands
> and fell about the chariot in showers,

> a lady came in view: an olive crown
> wreathed her immaculate veil, her cloak was green,
> the colors of live flame played on her gown.
>
> XXX

We are in the Earthly Paradise, and as we look up, we behold Beatrice descending in a shower of blossoms. Not only are we made to realize the space in which this takes place but— and this is extraordinary—we are compelled to take a fixed position as spectators of the scene, and thus we are not only brought into intimacy with it, but we are obliged to become aware of its beauty.

Dante, upon seeing Beatrice, is smitten by the force of love, that love which had already taken hold of his soul before his boyhood years had run their course. Dante turns to Virgil to reveal the state of his soul, but the "gentle father" has gone, and Dante cannot help but burst into tears.

Dante does not linger on Virgil's departure because he does not want to diminish the sacred atmosphere of the scene. The loud voice, rather the loud reproach of Beatrice shakes him, a reproach in which there is also a true love:

> ". . .For a while I stayed him
> with glimpses of my face. Turning my mild
>
> and youthful eyes into his very soul,
> I let him see their shining, and I led him
> by the straight way, his face to the right goal.
>
> The instant I had come upon the sill
> of my second age, and crossed and changed my life,
> he left me and let others shape his will.
> . . .
> He fell so far from every hope of bliss
> that every means of saving him had failed
> except to let him see the damned."
>
> XXX

Beatrice, stern, presses hard her reproach and Dante, weeping, confesses his faults.

The scene is the most autobiographical scene in the *Divine Comedy*. It is here that we get something very close to genuine self-revelation. Throughout the *Divine Comedy* Dante reveals himself through his characters, but here Dante discloses his true self very directly.

Now Matilda immerses Dante in the river Lethe so that he may drink the waters that wipe out all memory of sin:

> She had drawn me into the stream up to my throat,
> and pulling me behind her, she sped on
> over the water, light as any boat.
>
> XXXI

And the four cardinal virtues, the four maidens of Beatrice, and the three theological virtues, upon seeing Dante immersed in Lethe, beg Beatrice to turn her compassionate eyes to Dante:

> "Turn, Beatrice, oh turn the eyes of Grace,"
> was their refrain, "upon your faithful one
> who comes so far to look upon your face."
>
> XXXI

And the poet Dante bursts forth, exalting in Beatrice the "splendor of the eternal living light."

Now the chariot moves on. Dante beholds the tree of good and evil which represents the principle of obedience and, therefore, of the Empire. The griffon ties the pole of the chariot to the tree, and the tree immediately breaks into foliage. The members of the Heavenly pageant break into a song, unknown to mortals. Overpowered by the singing, Dante falls asleep.

Dante awakens and witnesses the allegory of the history of the Church and Italy abandoned by the emperor. The two Dantean motifs of religion and politics take the form of symbols, the eagle, the fox, the dragon, and the chariot, which becomes a seven-headed monster.

The full beauty of the contrast between religion and politics can hardly be enjoyed. It is hard to enjoy verses while we are wrestling with their meaning. Do the "seven heads" represent the seven deadly sins? Does the fox symbolize the heresies? It seems to me that in order to appreciate beauty or poetry, all the elements of appreciation must be present. There must be no interruption between the surface that Dante presents to us and the core.

In a few moments Dante will drink the waters of the river Eunoë with Statius. By drinking its waters every good is strengthened in Dante. Now Dante's final purification is completed, and he rises "perfect, pure and ready for the stars."   XXXIII

PARADISO

CHAPTER XVII

INTRODUCTION TO PARADISO.

The Paradise consists of nine spheres. Each sphere has its own history and exerts its own influence upon the destiny of man. The spheres will receive the blessed according to the attitude that has characterized their lives. Thus in Venus we find the amorous; in Mars the warriors. Here Dante accepts the pagan mythology and gives it a Christian imprint. It is the same procedure by which, according to Francesco Flora, "the pagan temples became Christian temples; and later on the poetry of the fourth *Eclogue* of Virgil was interpreted as predicting the coming of Christ."[1]

Each sphere is moved by heavenly beings, the Moon by the Angels, Mercury by the Archangels, Venus by the Principalities, the Sun by the Powers, Mars by the Virtues, Jupiter by the Dominations, Saturn by the Thrones, the Sphere of the Fixed Stars by the Cherubim, and the Primum Mobile by the Seraphim.

Dante's canticle is not disinterested. Dante has a philosophy to defend, a truth to proclaim. Dante celebrates virtuous women, holy emperors, great saints, saintly heroes, men of high purpose. He glorifies the nobility of man in the world of eternity.

Dante, who has now completed his much sought spiritual purification, is now in Paradise, the world of light.

Dante uses the word "light," "lume," in a sense that belongs explicitly to Christianity, a sense pertaining to mystical experience. When Dante speaks, as he does, of "light," we are apt to think of it as the expression of virtue or spirituality, whereas when he speaks of darkness we are apt to think of it as the expression of sin or matter. But the word "light" in Dante has much wider associations. It is now fire, now ardor, now flame, now lightning, now rainbow, now pearl, now emerald, now ruby. Dante makes use of these meanings to express the different moods of the blessed.

Dante brings to his view of light a sense of color developed and matured in the artistic Florentine atmosphere of his time. He differentiates the red color of the porphyry from that of the ruby, the orange color from the golden one, the whiteness of the snow from that of a pearl, the green of the new leaves from the green of the emerald. In discussing this keen sense of color, Francesco Flora has suggested that Dante "must have known the art of painting."[2]

Dante is certainly intoxicated with light or color. One cannot help wondering whether his eye disease—after all, he was a fervent devotee of St. Lucia, the patron of those with diseases of the eyes—had something to do with his emphasis on light or color. That is not to say that poor eyesight is itself enough to explain the nature of the *Paradiso*. But not seeing well must be considered in conjunction with Dante's person-

ality and character. A man who does not see well may be
more disposed to stress the world of light or color than a man
with normal eyesight who cannot appreciate its beauty with
the same intensity.

The Paradise is a world of dance. Dance expresses joy or
happiness.

Justinian and his companions (whom Dante and Beatrice
meet in the Heaven of Mercury) break into a hymn to the God
of Battles and, dancing, disappear into the distance:

> And all those souls joined in a holy dance,
> and then, like shooting sparks, gone instantly,
> they disappeared behind the veil of distance.
>
> VII

Dante and Beatrice reach the Sphere of Venus, and instantly
a band of souls that had been dancing in the Empyrean
descends to the travelers:

> No blast from cold clouds ever shot below,
> whether visible or not, so rapidly
> but what it would have seemed delayed and slow
>
> to one who had seen those holy lights draw nigh
> to where we were, leaving the dance begun
> among the Seraphim in Heaven on high.
>
> VIII

Beatrice and Dante meet St. Thomas Aquinas. They are
immediately surrounded by a garland of twelve souls. Aquinas identifies them and the souls dance around Dante and
Beatrice, raising their voices in harmonies unknown except
to Heaven itself:

> They stood like dancers still caught in the pleasure
> of the last round, who pause in place and listen
> till they have caught the beat of the new measure.
>
> X

In the Paradise, all the souls have a certain smile, "riso." Whether they meditate or reminisce, dance or sing, they always smile. Anyone who has read and meditated on the *Paradiso* will note the wonderful transformation that takes place when a soul smiles. The expanding presence that arises before us is no longer a mysterious or arcane figure. Through a smile, something of warm life comes back to the soul almost tinging its cheeks and lips. Let us consider the dialogue between Piccarda and Dante:

> "But tell me, please: do you who are happy here
> have any wish to rise to higher station,
> to see more, or to make yourselves more dear?"
>
> She smiled, as did the spirits at her side;
> then turning to me with such joy she seemed
> to burn with the first fire of love...
>
> III

Piccarda's smile, as well as the smile of all the souls in Paradise, is not the worldly, watchful, self-complacent smile of *Mona Lisa*. It is a smile that is the expression of noble sweetness and spiritual purity.

CHAPTER XVIII

PICCARDA. JUSTINIAN.

It is now noon. Beatrice raises her eyes up to the sun, "no eagle ever / stared at its shining with so fixed a gaze." Dante himself stares into the sun and sees it spark and blaze "like new-tapped iron when it pours white-hot."   I

> And suddenly, as it appeared to me,
> day was added to day, as if He who can
> had added a new sun to Heaven's glory.
>
>   I

And Dante sees and hears the music of the spheres, the harmony that God Himself controls. Dante is eager to know its cause. And Beatrice explains to him what he himself has not realized—that he and she are soaring toward the height of Heaven at an enormous speed. Having cast off all the

105

impurities from his soul, Dante rises effortlessly, without being aware of it at first, to his natural goal in the Godhead. Thus Beatrice and Dante reach the first sphere.

The first sphere is the sphere of the Moon, and here the souls who broke the holy vows appear to Dante as reflected images "in a still and limpid pool" or in a "clear glass when it is polished bright." The simplicity and clearness of these similes lift the reader to Dante's level of perception.   III

Here in the sphere of the Moon Dante encounters the soul of Piccarda Donati who explains to Dante the philosophy of the souls in Heaven. To Dante who is eager to know if the souls of an inferior sphere wish to rise to a higher station, Piccarda explains that every soul in Heaven rejoices in the entire will of God, and therefore desires no higher place than is assigned to it. To desire a higher place is to come into conflict with the will of God. Dante expresses this thought with some sublime verses:

> "In His will is our peace. It is that sea
> to which all moves, all that Itself creates
> and Nature bears through all Eternity."
>
>   III

How does Dante achieve this? Dante has theological and philosophical concerns, but his primary interest is the embodiment of these concerns in beautiful language.

Dante and Beatrice soar to the second sphere, the sphere of Mercury, inhabited by the seekers of honor:

> And like an arrow driven with such might
> it strikes its mark before the string is still,
> we soared to the second kingdom of the light.
>
>   V

The sphere shines more brightly because Beatrice glows with immense joy: "My lady glowed with such a joyous essence / ...that the planet shone more brightly with her presence."   V

Dante meets the emperor, Justinian, and the history of the Roman eagle (Empire) from the time of Aeneas, Caesar and Charlemagne to the time of Dante shines forth in Justinian's discourse. Dante, unlike St. Augustine, did not regard the Empire as the work of human pride and ambition but as a holy city especially created and ordained by God as the instrument of His divine purpose for the human race, and this is reflected in Justinian's discourse.

The verse becomes solemn and remote, delving into those remote and fatal times in which were forged the destinies of the world: "Once Constantine had turned the eagle's wing / against the course of Heaven, ..." Later on the verse becomes more of a narrative and ends with an invective against the Ghibellines (the aristocratic opposition party in Dante's Florence) who oppose the true purposes of the imperial eagle or the Holy Roman Empire:

> "Let them scheme, the Ghibellines, let them plot and weave
> under some other standard, for all who use
> this bird iniquitously find cause to grieve!"

VI

Dante and Beatrice reach the sphere of Venus, inhabited by the souls of the amorous. One of these souls identifies itself as Charles Martel of Anjou and prophesies dark days for the kingdom of Naples because of the meanness of king Robert, his brother. Dante asks Charles how it is that degenerate children can spring from noble parents. The king gives what seems an unsatisfactory answer: only by diversity of gifts can society function.

Dante encounters other souls such as Cunizza da Romano, Folquet of Marseilles and Rahab, a harlot of the city of Jericho, who hid Joshua's spies from the king's men and helped them to escape and whose soul now shines "like purest water lit by the sun's rays." IX

Dante and Beatrice ascend to the sphere of the Sun where they meet a garland of twelve souls. These souls are twelve doctors of the Church who surround Dante and Beatrice, as with a crown, and three times circle them, then pause, while one of them, Thomas Aquinas, begins to express his thoughts. When he has finished, the souls dance around Dante and Beatrice and begin to sing. Their song is like the early chime that wakes the monastery, calling the "well-ordered spirit" to prayer, and their various displays of love act and react among them in their perfect fellowship like the wheels and levers of a clock:

> Indi, come orologio che ne chiami
> nell'ora che la sposa di Dio surge
> a mattinar lo sposo perchè l'ami,
>
> che l'una parte l'altra tira e urge
> *tin tin* sonando con sì dolce nota,
> che'l ben disposto spirto d'amor turge;
>
> così vid'io la gloriosa rota
> muoversi e render voce a voce in tempra
> ed in dolcezza...
>
> Then as a clock tower calls us from above
> when the Bride of God rises to sing her matins
> to the Sweet Spouse, that she may earn his love,
>
> with one part pulling and another thrusting,
> *tin-tin*, so glad a chime the faithful soul
> swells with the joy of love almost to bursting—
>
> just so, I saw the wheel of glories start
> and chime from voice to voice in harmonies
> so sweetly joined,...

X

There is harmony among the souls, and the verses, with their musicality, reflect this harmony. The music of each verse is, so to speak, at point of intersection. It rises from its relation first to the verses immediately preceding and following it, and indefinitely to the rest of its context. Onomatopoeia and well-chosen words do the rest.

CHAPTER XIX

ST. FRANCIS. ST. DOMINIC. CACCIAGUIDA.

Dante, who was a true disciple of Thomas Aquinas, has Aquinas narrate the life of St. Francis of Assisi, from his birth to his wedding with Lady Poverty, from the approval of the Franciscan Rule to his mission to the Sultan, his stigmata, and finally to his death.

The language is splendid; common words become winged words. Francis' place of birth is not a simple village but the "fertile slope [that] spreads up the mountain's face"; Francis is not a mere friar but a prince sent by Providence to save the Church; Francis and Poverty are not companions but "lovers"; and his stigmata are not wounds but "Christ's final seal." What we normally hear in these words is the voice of the poet who has taken complete possession of his character. Dante brings the splendid character of St. Francis to life through his splendid diction.   XI

Now Dante is surrounded by a second garland of twelve souls. The spokesman of this second company is St. Bonaventure who eulogizes the life of St. Dominic from his birth in Calahorra ("the land to which the West wind, soft and glad, / returns each Spring to open the new leaves...") to his apostolic mission against the heretics ("like a torrent from a mountain vein, to smite / the stumps and undergrowths of heresy").   XII

Dante once more shows his poetic originality in his comparison of the garlands of souls to the rainbow:

> As through thin clouds or mists twin rainbows bend
> parallel arcs and equal coloring
> ...
>
> just so, those sempiternal roses wove
> their turning garland round us, and the outer
> answered the inner with the voice of love.
>
> XII

The average man does not really see things with his own eyes. He sees things through the eyes of others, be they painters or poets. He only sees in objects of man and nature those shapes and forms that the drawings and poems of the artists have put before him. But Dante's similes tell us that he is a direct student of nature.

Dante and Beatrice ascend and enter the fifth sphere, the sphere of Mars. This sphere is inhabited by the warriors of God who, by their light, form the sign of the Cross, which is the sign of victory. Here are Joshua, Charlemagne, Roland, Godfrey of Bouillon and Robert the Guiscard.

There is no more accomplished craftsman in the whole of European poetry than Dante. But to understand his verses fully, one should know that Dante was a poet who was also a student of philosophy and theology and a musician who wrote songs to be sung. This is very apparent in the following verses which describe the light of the souls of the warriors of God as a melody in its profound relations:

> And as a viol and a harp in a harmony
> of many strings, make only a sweet tinkle
> to one who has not studied melody;
>
> so from that choir of glories I heard swell
> so sweet a melody that I stood tranced,
> though what hymn they were singing, I could not tell.
>
> XIV

Here Dante develops the theme of Cacciaguida, who is Dante's great-great-grandfather and who followed Conrad in the Crusades, became a knight and died in battle, passing from martyrdom to bliss. The theme becomes intimate when Cacciaguida recalls the beautiful past. He recalls the frugal, domestic and chaste women of his time with great nostalgia:

> "One watched the cradle, babbling soft and low
> to soothe her child in the sweet idiom
> that is the first delight new parents know.
>
> Another, spinning in her simple home,
> would tell old tales to children gathered round her,
> of Troy and of Fiesole, and of Rome."
>
> XV

Cacciaguida expresses these thoughts with profound conviction, but obviously they find their germ in the mental life of Dante himself.

Dante is not a man who adapts himself easily to the change of social customs. He is one of those men who have a nostalgic turn of mind. These people believe that it is necessary to return to the past to avoid the problem of adjusting themselves to a new way of living. Dante hates the expansion of Florence with its ostentatious wealth, with its women hungry for adornment and pleasures, with its noise and tall buildings. Dante takes refuge in an ancient Florence with secure walls and chaste women—a Florence that existed only in his exaggerated imagination.

The theme of Cacciaguida is also connected with the ever recurring theme of exile, which is woven through the *Comedy*. It is Cacciaguida who prophesies Dante's exile:

> "All that you held most dear you will put by
> and leave behind you; and this is the arrow
> the longbow of your exile first lets fly.
>
> You will come to learn how bitter as salt and stone
> is the bread of others, how hard the way that goes
> up and down stairs that never are your own."
>
> XVII

These verses reveal Dante's personal sufferings, his dreadful fate—to be torn from his native city and turned loose upon the highways of the world. He was forced to travel to Verona, Lucca and Ravenna, a wanderer on earth, "having," says Daniel-Rops, "no homeland but his inner self where he accomplished a work of genius."[1] There is no doubt that Dante's exile helped him artistically. Without his exile his poetry would have been less poignant and moving. But Dante's exile, nevertheless, deprived him of everything dear to him, and caused him immense suffering.

The canto ends with Cacciaguida's encouragement of Dante. Though Dante fears offending important people with the publication of his *Comedy*, Cacciaguida bids him publish it because it will be a cry which, like the wind, will strike hardest at highest peaks, and this should be a source of honor:

> "Questo tuo grido farà come vento
> che le più alte cime percuote,
> e ciò non fia d'onor poco argomento."
>
> XVII

I quote the Italian verses because only they can express the proud, dedicated, impassioned tone of Cacciaguida's words. The reason is obvious. A thought expressed in a different language may be very close to the original, but the tone is not the same tone. A tone is too personal, too individual, unique, and it refuses to give up its own "personality" to the new language.

CHAPTER XX

THE EAGLE. THE VIRGIN MARY.

Dante turns back to Beatrice, sees her grow even more beautiful, and knows they have made the ascent to the sixth sphere of Jupiter, inhabited by the just and temperate rulers. The holy creatures fly by, singing "as birds arisen from a marshy plain" and form a spectacular arrangement of lights which spell out the message, letter by letter, "Love righteousness ye that are judges of the earth," "Diligite Iustitiam. Qui Iudicatis Terram." Then other holy creatures gather upon the crest of the last letter, twine round its limbs and form it into an eagle. The miraculous eagle speaks about the mystery of Divine Justice, which the human mind cannot penetrate. XVIII

Dante's representation of the eagle is not too artistic. He seems to reduce the whole scene to something not far removed from a circus. The reader is in danger of forgetting that this is Paradise, because his attention is drawn to something incongruously grotesque. But in spite of this, there is some great poetry when the eagle pauses briefly, and the spirits of the blessed sing a hymn, not as one symbolic entity, but each in its own voice:

> I seemed to hear a great flume take its course
> from stone to stone, and murmur down its mountain
> as if to show the abundance of its source.
>
> And as the sound emerging from a lute
> is tempered at its neck; and as the breath
> takes form around the openings of a flute—
>
> just so, allowing no delay to follow,
> the murmur of the eagle seemed to climb
> inside its neck, as if the neck were hollow.
>
> There it was given voice, and through the bill
> the voice emerged as words my heart awaited.

XX

The hymn ended, the eagle resumes speaking as one person. It identifies as chief souls of this sphere those splendors of which its eyes are composed: they are David, Ezekiel, Constantine, William of Sicily and the pagans Trajan and Ripheus. Dante cannot restrain the utterance of his amazement at the presence of these two pagans, and the eagle declares that both of them died in the true faith by a special grace of God, Ripheus in Christ to come and Trajan in Christ come. But the special grace of God, adds the eagle, is a mystery that man cannot understand.

Dante and Beatrice enter the sphere of Saturn, the sphere of the souls of the contemplative. Dante beholds a vision of a golden ladder on which countless splendors arise and descend like birds in flight.

Now Dante becomes very satirical about the ecclesiastics. Peter Damiano speaks with heavy satire about the clerics who neglect the world of contemplation and poverty, almost stunning the reader by its force of representation:

> "But now your pastors are so bloated and vain
> they go propped on either side, with a man before
> and another coming behind to bear the train.
>
> They cover even their mounts with the cloaks they wear
> so that two beasts move under a single hide.
> O Heavenly Patience, how long will you forebear!"
>
> XXI

Dante is a true satirical poet, and if satire had not existed before him he would have invented it. If his soul needed poetry, his talent needed invective. Dante was one of those men who are harshly sensitive. They always feel strongly and see clearly in the world what is causing their suffering, and they concentrate with a vengeance on its documentation.

From the sphere of Saturn Dante looks down through the seven spheres and wonders at the insignificance of earth:

> My eyes went back through the seven spheres below,
> and I saw this globe, so small, so lost in space,
> I had to smile at such a sorry show.
>
> Who thinks it the least pebble in the skies
> I most approve. . .
>
> And all the seven, in a single view,
> showed me their masses, their velocities,
> and the distances between each in its purlieu.
>
> And turning there with the eternal Twins,
> I saw the dusty little threshing ground
> that makes us ravenous for our mad sins,
>
> saw it from mountain crest to lowest shore.
>
> XXII

Dante has a hierarchical view of the universe. The earth is only a small fraction of the real world, and it is surrounded on every side by the eternal world, like an island in the ocean. But though the earth is insignificant in Dante's vision of the universe, it is nevertheless very important to him. Whatever takes place in Florence, in Italy and in Europe is of great concern to the souls in Hell and Purgatory, as well as to the saints in Paradise, and says Christopher Dawson, "the divine pageant in the Earthly Paradise which is the center of the whole process is an apocalyptic vision of the judgment and reformation of the Church and the Empire in the fourteenth century."[1]

Dante and Beatrice ascend to the eighth sphere or the sphere of the Fixed Stars, the sphere of the triumphant splendors, of the triumph of Christ. Beatrice stares expectantly toward that part of the sky where the sun (the divine Illumination) is at its highest point, like a mother bird that, after covering her beloved young in her nest all through the night, is eager for the dawn so that she may hunt for food for her fledglings.

In this sphere of the Fixed Stars shines the mother of Christ, the Virgin Mary, and around her revolves the angel Gabriel. Dante describes Gabriel's praise of the Lady of Heaven who follows her son in this way:

> The sweetest strain that ever swelled aloud
> to draw the soul into itself down here,
> would be as thunder from a shattered cloud,
>
> compared to the melody that then aspired
> from the bright lyre that crowned the purest gem
> by which the brightest heaven is ensapphired.

XXIII

This praise culminates in the image of the splendors who, to express their love for Mary, extend their flames on high, a brilliant image that changes the religious emotion into an act of faith.

CHAPTER XXI

THE APOSTLES. BEATRICE.

In the sphere of the Fixed Stars Dante is examined by St. Peter, the first custodian of the Church, on faith, and then by St. James and St. John on hope and charity. It is a necessary rite so that Dante may be worthy of the vision of God; it is an interview about religious doctrine in the form of questions and answers; it is a colloquium between the priest and the catechuman that constitutes the very nature of catechism:

> "Speak, good Christian, manifest your worth:
> what is faith?"
> . . .
> "Faith is the *substance* of what we hope to see
> and the *argument* for what we have not seen."
>
> XXIV

118

Dante attaches importance to edification. One cannot have the final vision of God unless his faith is firm and secure. Edification, a poetry that teaches, has become the object of derision now. That poetry should teach or inculcate religion seems to most people incompatible with its true function. But it is clear that Dante, even when he teaches religion, intersperses his teaching with true poetry.

Do we need some instances? St. James examines Dante on hope, and Dante answers: " 'Hope,' I said, 'is the certain expectation / of future glory. It is the blessed fruit / of grace divine and the good a man has done.' " St. John rises to examine Dante on charity "as a joyous maid will rise and go / to join the dance." Dante has a great facility of phrase, and it may be observed that, when other poets have borrowed from him or have arrived independently at the same simile, it is usually Dante who has the best of it.   XXV

Now before Dante appears a great splendor, which Beatrice identifies as the soul of Adam. Dante quivers with emotion:

> As a bough that bends its crown to the wind's course,
> and then, after the blow, rises again
> uplifted by its own internal force;
>
> so did I as she spoke, all tremulous;
> then calmed again, assured by a desire
> to speak that burned in me....

XXVI

Dante begs Adam to speak, and learns from him that the world was created two thousand years before Christ; that Adam was in Eden for six hours; that Adam spoke the language spoken by Nimrod and his people before they were stricken at the Tower of Babel.

Here again is a return of Dante's theme condemning the corruption of the clergy. Now St. Peter glows red with righteous indignation, as he denounces the evil doings of the popes. All Heaven darkens at this tale of shame. St. Peter charges the papacy with becoming acquisitive, political and therefore bloody:

> "The bride of Christ was not suckled of old
> on blood of mine, of Linus, and of Cletus
> to be reared as an instrument for grabbing gold.
>
> It was to win this life of blessedness
> Sixtus, and Pius, and Calixtus, and Urban
> let flow the blood and tears of their distress.
>
> We never meant that men of Christian life
> should sit part on the right, part on the left
> of our successors, steeled for bloody strife."
>
> XXVII

Moral indignation may make poetry, but it must be indignation recollected in tranquillity. In these verses, to borrow a T. S. Eliot concept,[1] a feigned indignation is presented, instead of a real indignation being recalled. The total effect is one of querulousness. The indictment of the whole history of the Church since the third century fails. It is incredible that, during all these intervening centuries, Dante cannot find a holy or sympathetic pope. Dante utters generalizations, and generalizations are seldom true. What keeps the verses alive at all is the undercurrent of personal bitterness caused by Dante's hardships experienced at the hands of the Church.

Now the blessed soar away, and Dante is left with Beatrice who tells him to look down. Dante looks down, and he sees the earth as an insignificant mote in space. He once more turns his thoughts upward as Beatrice leads him in the ascent to the ninth sphere, the Primum Mobile.

Here Dante gives a beautiful vesture to the problem of space.

> "The order of the universe, whose nature
> holds firm the center and spins all else around it,
> takes from this heaven its first point of departure.

This heaven does not exist in any place
but in God's mind, where burns the love that turns it
and the power that rains to it from all of space."

XXVII

Dante also gives beautiful expression to the very difficult
problem of time. The human days and years spring like a
plant, with roots and leaves, from God's mind:

"So may you understand how time's taproot
is hidden in this sphere's urn, while in the others
we see its spreading foliage and its fruit."

XXVII

But if the discussion of the problem of space and time is
poetic, Dante's representation of God's creation of the angels
is both beautiful and original. The angels become "pure
essences," "new loves...born of Eternal Love:"

"In His eternity, beyond time, above
all other comprehension, as it pleased Him,
new loves were born of the Eternal love.

Nor did He lie asleep before the Word
sounded above these waters; 'before' and 'after'
did not exist until His voice was heard.

Pure essence, and pure matter, and the two
joined into one were shot forth without flaw,
like three bright arrows from a three-string bow."

XXIX

Dante has his own language, as well as his own creative
imagination and poetic technique, and if one or two of these
elements are derived from the Bible, they are enriched with a
new substance and beauty. Besides phrases, there are many
words and similes which Dante has borrowed from the Bible,
but they are always originally developed. They move from
the traditional source to acquire an unexpected individuality.

CHAPTER XXII

THE MYSTIC ROSE. ST. BERNARD.

Dante and Beatrice are now in the Empyrean or the city of God. Beatrice is at last at home. Her beauty is now perfect, and Dante praises her lavishly.

Beatrice promises Dante a vision of both hosts of Paradise, the soldiery of the blessed and the soldiery of the angels. Dante is blinded by a new radiance, hears a voice announce that he shall be given new powers, and immediately sees a vision of a river of light flowing between enameled banks with the angels and the blessed diving into it:

> I saw a light that was a river flowing
> light within light between enameled banks
> painted with blossoms of miraculous spring;

and from the river as it glowed and rolled
live sparks shot forth to settle on the flowers.
They seemed like rubies set in bands of gold;

and then, as if the fragrance overthrew
their senses, they dove back into the river;
and as one dove in there, out another flew.

XXX

In the presence of this imagery, we feel transported to a
world where there are no sordid cares, no struggles. It is a
world of great purity, grace and loveliness.

Dante pictures the Empyrean or divine city as a mystic
rose, whose tiers of petals hold the blessed, while the angels
soar above the rose, like Heavenly bees in constant motion
between the rose and the radiance of God:

Then, in the form of a white rose, the host
of the sacred soldiery appeared to me,
all those whom Christ in his own blood espoused.

But the other host (who soar, singing and seeing
His glory, who to will them to his love
made them so many in such blissful being

like a swarm of bees who in one motion dive
into the flowers, and in the next return
the sweetness of their labors to the hive)

flew ceaselessly to the many-petaled rose
and ceaselessly returned into that light
in which their ceaseless love has its repose.

Like living flame their faces seemed to glow.
Their wings were gold. And all their bodies shone
more dazzling white than any earthly snow.

On entering the great flower they spread about them,
from tier to tier, the ardor and the peace
they had acquired in flying close to Him.

XXXI

Dante has enshrined noble tenderness, human sublimity, pure love, all the blessings and magnificence of Christianity in these verses, and they are so radiant that one can often return to them to renew inspiration.

In Paradise Beatrice has resumed her throne among the blessed. Across the vastness of Paradise, Dante sends his soul's prayer to Beatrice. It is a prayer in which Dante thanks Beatrice for helping him find his road to salvation:

> "O lady in whom my hope shall ever soar
> and who for my salvation suffered even
> to set your feet upon Hell's broken floor;
>
> through your power and your excellence alone
> have I recognized the goodness and the grace
> inherent in the things I have been shown.
>
> You have led me from my bondage and set me free
> by all those roads, by all those loving means
> that lay within your power and charity.
>
> Grant me your magnificence that my soul,
> which you have healed, may please you when it slips
> the bonds of flesh and rises to its goal."
>
> XXXI

Dante's prayer is followed by that of St. Bernard. The great saint begs the Virgin Mary to intercede in Dante's behalf so that he may be allowed the direct vision of God:

> "Virgin Mother, daughter of thy son;
> humble beyond all creatures and more exalted;
> predestined turning point of God's intention;
>
> thy merit so ennobled human nature
> that its divine Creator did not scorn
> to make Himself the creature of His creature.
> . . .

And I, who never more desired to see
the vision myself than I do that he may see It,
add my own prayer, and pray that it may be

enough to move you to dispel the trace
of every mortal shadow by thy prayers
and let him see revealed the Sum of Grace..."

XXXIII

Dante wrote a sublime prayer in spite of artistic difficulty.
To write verses is easy, but to write religious verses is very
difficult because the feeling the poet expresses must be something that can be completely shared. Dante fully succeeds in
this; and if we place him alongside the traditional writers of
religious verses, such as St. Thomas Aquinas and St.
Ambrose, Dante is certainly superior. He elevates common
language to greatness with the final touch of genius.

St. Bernard's prayer is answered. From that moment
Dante looks into the eternal light and begins to understand
its power and majesty. There is no power in Dante capable of
speaking the truth of what he sees; yet the impress of the
truth is stamped upon his soul forever:

As one who sees in dreams and wakes to find
the emotional impression of his vision
still powerful while its parts fade from his mind—

just such am I, having lost nearly all
the vision itself, while in my heart I feel
the sweetness of it yet distill and fall.

So, in the sun, the footprints fade from snow.
On the wild wind that bore the tumbling leaves
the Sybil's oracles were scattered so.

XXXIII

The canto is sublime because of the beauty of its language,
uplifting tone and similes but also because it touches the
reader's soul at its vital core. The reader's soul is touched by

Dante's intense desire to know the nature of God: a desire which cannot be satisfied because of man's limited nature.

Before this dramatic spectacle we are overwhelmed by a feeling of profound awe, almost bewilderment, a sense that we are very close to the secret of Dante's soul and, therefore, of the *Divine Comedy*: the deeply felt desire to know the nature of God. This very desire, a cry which rises toward Heaven and which moves us greatly, is what gives the canto and the *Divine Comedy* a hold on the divine.

NOTES

Preface

[1] Quoted by Henry Daniel-Rops, *Cathedral and Crusade*, Garden City, Doubleday Co., 1963, Vol. II, p.381.

[2] Quoted by Daniel-Rops, ibid., p.383.

[3] See Attilio Momigliano, *Storia della letteratura italiana*, Milano, Giuseppe Principato, 1962, p.45.

Chapter I

[1] Concetto Marchesi, *Storia della letteratura latina*, Milano, Giuseppe Principato, 1979, Vol. I, p.454.

[2] Joseph Pieper, *The Four Cardinal Virtues*, South Bend, Notre Dame University Press, 1966, p.10.

[3] T.S. Eliot, *On Poetry and Poets*, New York, Farrar, Strauss & Giroux, 1973, p.205.

[4] Eugenio Donadoni, *Breve storia della letteratura italiana*, Milano, Signorelli, 1968, p.56.

Chapter II

[1] Francesco Flora, *Storia della letteratura italiana*, Milano, Arnoldo Mondadori, 1967, Vol. I, p.161.

[2] *Ibid.*, p.162.

Chapter III

[1]   Henry Daniel-Rops, *Cathedral*, op. cit., p.385.
[2]   Quoted by John Dover Wilson in *The Essential Shakespeare*, London, Cambridge University Press, 1964, p.82.
[3]   Francesco Flora, *op. cit.*, p.165.

Chapter V

[1]   Francesco Flora, *op. cit.*, p.169.

Chapter VI

[1]   John O. Sinclair, *Dante's Inferno*, New York, Oxford University Press, 1961, p.223.

Chapter VII

[1]   Quoted by Louis Untermeyer in *Lives of the Poets*, New York, Simon & Schuster, 1959, p.675.

Chapter XII

[1]   John D. Sinclair, *Dante's Purgatorio*, New York, Oxford University Press, 1961, p.129.

Chapter XVI

[1]   Bernard Berenson, *Italian Painters of the Renaissance*, New York, World Publishing, 1971, p.318.

Chapter XVII

[1]   Francesco Flora, *op. cit.*, p.196.
[2]   Ibid., p.195.

Chapter XIX

[1]   Henry Daniel-Rops, *Cathedral*, op. cit., p.383.

Chapter XX

[1]   Christopher Dawson, *The Dynamics of World History*, edit. by John Mulloy, New York, The New American Library, 1962, p.240.

Chapter XXI

[1]   T.S. Eliot, *On Poetry*, op. cit., p.205.